A

Supply Chain Management

Guide to

Business Continuity

Betty A. Kildow, CBCP, FBCI

AMACOM

American Management Association

New York • Atlanta • Brussels • Chicago • Mexico City • San Francisco
Shanghai • Tokyo • Toronto • Washington, D.C.

This publication is designed to provide accurate and authoritative information in regard to the subject matter covered. It is sold with the understanding that the publisher is not engaged in rendering legal, accounting, or other professional service. If legal advice or other expert assistance is required, the services of a competent professional person should be sought.

Library of Congress Cataloging-in-Publication Data

Kildow, Betty A.
    A supply chain management guide to business continuity / Bettty A. Kildow. — 1st ed.
        p. cm.
    Includes bibliographical references and index.
    ISBN-13: 978-0-8144-1645-7
    ISBN-10: 0-8144-1645-4
    1. Business logistics. I. Title.
    HD38.5.K476 2011
    658.1'6—dc22
                                                                    2010018553

About AMA
American Management Association (www.amanet.org) is a world leader in talent development, advancing the skills of individuals to drive business success. Our mission is to support the goals of individuals and organizations through a complete range of products and services, including classroom and virtual seminars, webcasts, webinars, podcasts, conferences, corporate and government solutions, business books and research. AMA's approach to improving performance combines experiential learning—learning through doing—with opportunities for ongoing professional growth at every step of one's career journey.

Printing number

10 9 8 7 6 5 4 3 2 1

This book is dedicated to my wonderful family, especially Terry for his support, understanding, and willing horse-holding; Kent and Wyatt, each loved always and ever as they travel disparate paths; and Sebastian and Annaleise, two very awesome people I am blessed to have in my life.

Contents

Foreword

RISK MANAGEMENT, in the cloak of business continuity, must be on the radar screen of every business management team—from "top to bottom." From planning to documentation, from risk identification to hazard assessment, from global business continuity strategies to the key role of supply management, this book is full of practical, relevant, step-by-step approaches for managing the unknown.

It's abundantly clear that this book was written with several audiences in mind, and virtually anyone with business management and especially supply chain responsibilities will find value in the various chapters of *this* information-packed book. Written in an easy-to-read style, the book covers the basics, and goes on to explore strategies and best practices, regulations and requirements, tools for identifying and managing risks, and tools for planning and analysis. It also includes a glossary and several appendices that readers will find helpful.

If you want examples, checklists, and horror stories to make your point for business recovery planning, you will find them here. And, each chapter ends nicely with recommended specific actions to move the business continuity process forward and make the results more effective.

A Supply Chain Management Guide to Business Continuity provides another convincing case for enduring focus on all matters with the outcome " . . . of the organization to provide service and support for its customers to maintain its viability before, during, and after a disaster." For all supply management professionals in a quest to understand and mitigate risk in today's dynamic business environment, this book is a real find.

Paul Novak, CPSM, C.P.M., MCIPS
Chief Executive Officer
Institute for Supply Management™

Acknowledgments

MY GRATITUDE and warm thanks are due to the great team at AMACOM with whom I was fortunate to collaborate while working on this book: Bob Nirkind, who deserves tremendous recognition for understanding and believing in the importance of the topic and for his wise counsel and insight; Mike Sivilli for expertly shepherding the book from original manuscript to completion with a small miracle or two along the way; and Jackie Laks Gorman for her eagle eye and highly skilled copyediting. Your combined talents helped make this book more readable and of more value to its readers than I could have ever done on my own.

Introduction

WHETHER YOUR BUSINESS is large or small, whether your company manufactures printed circuit boards or plastic molding machines or sells handbags or lawn furniture, it is not unreasonable to expect that there is a crisis looming some time in its future. The reality is that no business or industry is immune from crisis. While our tendency is to think about major disasters that create havoc and impact whole communities—such as earthquakes, hurricanes, floods, or severe winter storms—for most businesses, the disaster is more likely to be on a smaller scale. For most businesses, disaster can come from an event that may not generate headlines, such as a water main break in the immediate area, a fire confined to a small section of their business, or the failure of their IT systems.

And though we tend to think in terms of environmental disruptions, such as natural catastrophes or pandemics, we must also consider social disruptions (strikes, sabotage), technical disruptions (a breakdown of equipment, loss of a key skilled staff member), political disruptions (terrorist attacks, civil unrest, nationalization), legal disruptions (legal shutdowns, injunctions), and economic disruptions (supplier failure, exchange rate fluctuations, takeovers).

Just as it is not possible to totally prevent most disasters and disruptions, it is not realistic to assume that they will happen to other organizations but not to yours. Being prepared when the things that "can never happen here" do happen is just plain good business. Failure to plan for such events can lead to supply chain disruptions that can devastate company performance, damage profitability and stock prices, and result in irreparable harm to the organization. The consequences can also result in cascading damage to every business and organization relying on the timely receipt of your goods or services that enable them to continue meeting their customers' needs in order to generate revenue and protect their bottom line. Who wants to stand in front of a board of directors, senior executives, or a major customer in the wake of unsuccessful attempts to restore critical operations following a disaster? Who wants to respond to their queries about why the threat went undetected, why an identified risk was not eliminated or mitigated, or why strategies were not in place to enable the organization to get back on its feet quickly?

The Effects of a Disaster

In today's global economy, the effects of a disaster can be more than just local; its impact can reach across country borders and oceans. In 1995, a magnitude 7.2 earthquake struck Kobe, Japan, resulting in 5,100 deaths and devastating physical destruction. Following the earthquake, all area steel mills were shut down and many other businesses became nonoperational as a result of water and gas outages. Secondary business and supply chain interruptions were extensive. Kobe was Japan's biggest international trade hub and a major production and logistics center, with approximately 30 percent of Japan's shipping passing through it. Even businesses with no direct physical impact suffered because of damage to the utilities, port, railroads, and roads. Production was impossible, and shipments in or out were difficult to unachievable. When Sumitomo's Metal Industries Ltd.—the sole source of brake shoes for Toyota—closed its plant in nearby Osaka, most of Toyota's plants in other parts of Japan closed as well. For companies like Toyota that used a just-in-time (JIT) inventory management system and relied on frequent shipments of parts and materials, there was little available inventory on hand, leading to an interruption of production. According to published estimates, Toyota lost $200 million in revenue. Moreover, the disaster cascaded and caused supply chain interruptions for businesses in other parts of the world, including U.S. companies IBM and Apple, which relied on displays produced in Kobe.

Even a seemingly relatively small emergency can result in a large business disruption. In 2000, a Phillips microchip manufacturing plant in New Mexico was struck by lightning, creating a small fire. Though quickly extinguished, the fire caused contamination in the sterile manufacturing facility, contaminated millions of chips, and halted the chip-making process. The company's two primary customers were the two largest mobile phone companies in Europe, which used chips manufactured at the plant in cellular telephones. One of the companies, Nokia, became immediately aware of the disruption in chip deliveries and acted quickly, working closely with the chip manufacturer. Nokia arranged to purchase chips from another of its primary supplier's plants as well as other alternative sources, quickly tying up the spare capacity. Some phone models were even re-engineered to allow the use of chips from yet other suppliers. With pre-disaster plans in place, Nokia was able to continue to assemble and distribute its products and gain a greater market share. On the other hand, Ericsson—the other mobile phone company affected—purchased all its microchips parts from the single source to simplify its supply chain. Ericsson did not respond quickly enough, had no supply chain continuity plan in place to obtain the chips, already in short supply, from another source; and suffered a lengthy and costly disruption in its assembly and distribution processes. The resulting inability to launch new products, loss of market share, and financial losses in the hundreds of millions of dollars made it necessary for Ericsson to merge with another company just to survive. The overall outcome was a permanent shift in the balance of power between the two electronics giants.

Mishaps such as technological failures—even those that occur outside the organization—can become an inherited disaster. When a major power outage started shortly after 4:00 P.M. EDT on Thursday, August 14, 2003, within three minutes, twenty-one power plants shut down, impacting eight states—including New York, New Jersey, Ohio, Michigan, Connecticut, and Pennsylvania—and parts of Canada, including Ontario. Estimates of the total cost of the blackout have ranged from $4 billion to $10 billion in lost income to workers and investors, extra costs to government agencies, repair costs to the impacted utilities, and costs for lost or spoiled food and other commodities.

Consider what a similar power outage would mean for your organization. Approximately one-fourth of the businesses hit by the outage reported that their resulting losses were more than $40,000 per hour of resulting downtime, and some indicated they lost more than $1 million each hour there was no power. Some companies reported that the outage disrupted deliveries from suppliers and deliveries to customers. In Michigan, cascading consequences were reported even outside the blacked-out area as a result of delayed and extended delivery times for parts and materials, particularly disrupting for manufacturing operations with JIT scheduling.

Taking the Necessary Steps

In managing risk, there are three fundamental truths:

1. Only a working crystal ball would enable us to predict all the risks that our organization might face in the future.
2. We cannot fully control risks.
3. By developing and maintaining an enterprise-wide business continuity program that includes all internal and external components of the supply chain, we can prepare to manage risks in order to continue meeting stakeholder expectations when disasters occur.

If we can agree that disasters are inevitable, it would seem logical that we must also agree that it is wise to take the necessary steps to manage our risks to the extent possible and to reduce the effects of disruptions through planning and preparedness.

In my work with clients, I have undertaken the mission of integrating the internal and external supply chain links in continuity planning, and it has often been a hard sell. Fortunately, that is changing as there has been a realization that the supply chain from procurement through delivery is the revenue source for most companies and is directly tied to cash flow, profitability, growth, and the related intangibles such as protection of the brand, customer trust, and stakeholder confidence.

There is a growing awareness that a disaster that impacts the supply chain is a disaster for the entire company. Incidents affecting the supply chain were often overlooked in earlier business continuity planning, but this is changing. One indication of the increasing realization of the vulnerability of today's supply chains and the importance of fully including the supply chain in all aspects of risk management, including business continuity, came at the Institute for Supply Management (ISM)'s 95th Annual International Supply Management Conference and Educational Exhibit, held in April 2010. The conference included a risk management track with daily workshops focused on connecting risk management to supply chain management. In addition, the four-day event offered two half-day sessions dedicated to business continuity and the supply chain.

I have specialized in business continuity, disaster recovery, and emergency management consulting for twenty years. I have been a Certified Business Continuity Professional with the Disaster Continuity Institute since 1998 and a fellow of the Business Continuity Institute since 2002. I've worked with utility companies, luxury fashion goods companies, a hot sauce manufacturer, a PVC pipe manufacturer, a division of a car manufacturer, and government agencies, among other organizations. I've watched as business continuity has matured to become what it is today, and I have witnessed what works—and what doesn't—when developing and maintaining a successful continuity program. In *A Supply Chain Management Guide to Business Continuity*, I want to pass along my lessons learned by providing a resource for all those who want to better manage supply chain risks. I would also like to raise awareness of the importance of business continuity planning as an enterprise-wide issue that must include the supply chain to fulfill its purpose.

My goal is to provide an easy-to-read, easy-to-understand book that focuses on supply chain business continuity within the framework of an overall business continuity program. While the terminology used is corporate-centric, the principles and planning methods can be applied in all types of organizations, large and small, including not-for-profits and government agencies.

How This Book Is Organized

To lay a foundation and level the playing field, the book begins in Chapter 1 with business continuity basics and the evolution of business continuity planning. A discussion of business continuity ownership and drivers and where continuity planning fits in the bigger picture of managing an organization's risks follows in Chapter 2. Current best practices are outlined in Chapter 3, with an overview of the business continuity planning lifecycle and its application in the development of a continuity program that incorporates the four components needed to successfully manage business risks. Chapter 4 discusses an enterprise-wide approach to risk management that integrates all elements of the supply chain, from purchasing through distribution, and recommends the need to honestly assess current disaster management capabilities.

Building on the basic steps introduced in Chapter 3, a sequential process to carry out each step of the planning lifecycle is detailed in the chapters that follow:

→ Conducting a hazard assessment (Chapter 5)

→ Performing a business impact analysis (Chapter 6)

→ Developing supply chain business continuity strategies (Chapter 7)

→ Writing actionable business continuity plan documents (Chapter 8)

→ Providing people with continuity training and testing plans and performing ongoing maintenance for a successful business continuity program (Chapter 9)

The process is one I have applied when working with a broad range of clients, and I know it can work.

Finally, Chapter 10 offers an overview of current business continuity standards, regulations, and requirements, as well as certification programs for business continuity programs and continuity practitioners. The chapter examines some of the ways to validate and certify your own program and that of a supplier or other business partner.

Each chapter concludes with a "Going Forward" feature that suggests specific action items that, when followed, can help you gain a more comprehensive understanding of your organization's current business continuity capability. There may also be initial steps to begin development of a new business continuity program or to enhance an existing one.

Following the last chapter is a Glossary that includes definitions and acronyms for some of the commonly used words and terminology related to both business continuity and the supply chain that you will find in this book. There are also five appendices, which are tools to assist you in carrying out the steps of the continuity planning lifecycle:

- → A business continuity planning assessment questionnaire for use in conducting an initial assessment of your organization's current level of continuity preparedness
- → A checklist of general and supply chain–specific hazards to initiate a hazard assessment
- → A guide to use in pandemic planning
- → Guidance for establishing a business continuity organization, with five continuity team models and tips for selecting continuity team members
- → Sample outlines for a corporate business continuity plan and a business unit continuity plan, as well as a sample basic department business continuity plan

Who This Book Is For

Because many areas of an organization have a role to play in business continuity and must work in concert to develop and maintain a capability to manage risk, this book has been written for many audiences, all of whom have a vested interest in their organization's supply chain and the ability of that supply chain to continue to function smoothly. For supply chain professionals—who may be assigned responsibility for developing those portions of a corporate business continuity plan that address their business unit or be asked to create department-specific continuity strategies or perhaps a supply chain annex (i.e., appendix) to a business continuity plan—this book will provide a basic real-world understanding of business continuity that will lead to them asking pertinent questions about their organization's business continuity planning and to better understand the answers they receive. Some of the questions these people need to ask are: What is business continuity really all about? How vulnerable is our supply chain? What considerations are critical to developing effective supply chain continuity strategies and plans? What can I do to improve our disaster capability?

For supply chain managers not assigned to business continuity responsibilities, the book presents guidelines to consider in determining whether their business unit has been accurately and sufficiently included in the organization's business continuity program. These people need to ask: Is our organization vulnerable as a result of not including my department's business functions in the business continuity program? Are there things I can do unilaterally that will lessen some of our risks and plug some of the gaps in our business continuity strategies?

For purchasing and procurement managers, who can play a huge role in helping to prevent potential disasters, this book can offer some food for thought and specific things to look for when selecting suppliers and contractors. These people need to ask: Have we included risk factors in our review of potential suppliers? How prepared are our primary suppliers, outsourcing companies, and shippers to manage their own disasters? Are there opportunities to collaborate with business partners in continuity planning?

For those responsible for disaster recovery—the technology piece of business continuity—such as the director of IT or the disaster recovery manager, this book can provide greater insight into supply chain continuity. As a result, these individuals may see a need for better support and more rapid recovery of supply chain technology following a disaster. These people need to ask: Does restoration of supply chain–related systems need to be moved up on our recovery priority list? Do we need to do some further recovery testing of supply chain applications?

For risk managers, the book can be used to review supply chain risks to help ensure that all enterprise vulnerabilities are identified and addressed. These people need to ask: Is our current business interruption insurance appropriate to our supply chain risks? Do our loss control strategies address all risks, including those of a leaner supply chain?

For business continuity managers who have overall responsibility for developing and maintaining comprehensive enterprise-wide continuity programs, this book can provide a more supply chain–specific view of continuity management. Equally important is opening the door for more effective collaboration among business continuity planners and supply chain managers. These people need to ask: Are there supply chain gaps in our plans? Do we need to revisit the planning process to more fully incorporate all supply chain risks, internal and external? Would our business continuity planning group be strengthened by adding knowledgeable supply chain representation?

And finally, for top level executives, the book can offer a more in-depth understanding of their company's business continuity program and what is necessary to manage risks throughout the organization. These people need to ask: Does the program fully support the organization's mission statement? Is the current business continuity reporting structure the most effective for our organization? Would I be comfortable and confident standing in front of our board of directors, owners, stockholders, or the communities we serve and touting the fact that we are fully ready to meet the demands a disaster may place on our organization and its operations?

Does this book fully cover all the most current information? Yes and no. While there can be no definitive book on the subject of business continuity, as of the date the final word was written, this book was a snapshot from my viewpoint of business continuity today. Yet it is quite likely that between then and the day you read this, changes have occurred, both in emergent disaster threats throughout the world that may result in new supply chain risks and in the continuing evolution of the many aspects of business continuity planning, and those changes may provide new risk management approaches or more stringent business continuity requirements.

To a varying degree, each person involved in the challenging pursuit of business continuity planning might view their assigned planning role as a mission as we plan for events usually outside our control that everyone hopes and prays will never happen.

Steps taken now to fully address supply chain issues in your company's proactive approach to managing disasters will help ensure that the needs and expectations of customers are met and that the organization's good reputation remains intact with all stakeholders.

We are all customers; we are all suppliers.

CHAPTER 1

Business Continuity Basics

A S A RESULT of catastrophic natural and human-caused disasters that have occurred over the past two decades, coupled with increasingly stringent regulatory requirements, the interest in and need for business continuity has never been greater. For a large corporation or a small to medium-size enterprise, a business continuity program produces a level of resilience that enables the continuity or quick resumption of operations following any disaster. It is this capacity that ensures an organization's ability to safeguard the interests of stakeholders, stay competitive, and comply with regulatory requirements. In some cases, business continuity can mean the difference between life and death for an organization.

Supply chains are the lifeblood of organizations. This is most obvious for retailers, wholesalers, distributors, and manufacturers. However, it is equally true for all other types of companies and businesses, whether they are private sector, public sector, or not-for-profits, as well as for government agencies. And, while the product itself is different from that of companies that produce and deliver a tangible commodity, service providers also have their own supply chains in the delivery of their service to customers.

Linking organizations, industries, and even economies, these arteries of business are extremely complex. Although we think in terms of the generally accepted terminology *supply chain*, the terms *supply network* or *supply chain system* better describe these multifaceted operations. In today's demand-driven supply chains, products and information are rapidly flowing, at times simultaneously and concurrently, in order to ensure that products and services are delivered in the correct quantities, to the right place at the right time, at the required quality levels, and with the ongoing requirement that everything always be done economically. As customers, we require it. As suppliers and service providers, it is our company's mission.

To omit the supply chain from business continuity planning is to omit the arteries that deliver the lifeblood to all business operations and make it possible to produce and distribute our commodities and services and thus meet customer needs and requirements. If business continuity plans do not include strategies for continuing or rapidly restoring supply chain operations following a disaster or otherwise significant interruption of operations, it is almost a certainty that restoration of operations will be delayed or halted as an ad hoc approach is taken to reestablishing the supply chain.

What Business Continuity Is . . . and Is Not

There is not yet one meaning of business continuity that is understood, accepted, and applied universally. There are both theoretical and the functional definitions, and the lines between them often become blurred. Chief among these are the definitions of business continuity and disaster recovery, which even today are often used almost interchangeably.

For purposes of the discussions in this book, I use the following definition of *business continuity*, which is one of the most commonly accepted definitions: A proactive approach to ensure continuity or rapid restoration of delivery of the organization's service or product following a disaster; the ability of an organization to provide service and support for its customers and to maintain its viability before, during, and after a disaster.

Beyond a dictionary definition, business continuity is:

→ A proactive approach to managing operational risks
→ A program focused on protecting the organization's brand by ensuring its excellent reputation for reliability
→ A strategic framework for improving an organization's resilience to disaster-caused interruptions
→ A set of strategies for keeping the most critical business functions running while normal operations are restored
→ The plan and procedure to enable the timely and orderly continuation of or rapid restoration of operations following a disaster
→ A well-developed and maintained program with a goal of minimizing service and delivery delays and helping to ensure that customer and other stakeholder expectations are met
→ Part of a multifaceted approach to protect the organization from risks
→ An enterprise-wide management issue
→ Activity performed by or on behalf of an organization to ensure that critical business functions are available to customers, suppliers, regulators, and other stakeholders that need or require access to those functions
→ Excellent and prudent business management

To further define business continuity, it may also be helpful to acknowledge some misconceptions—things that business continuity is not. For example, business continuity is not:

→ *Business as Usual*. It is business in survival mode or fight for your continued existence mode. The sole goal is to maintain an acceptable level of operation to fulfill the organization's primary mission. The bells, whistles, frills, and ribbons we all love and take for granted are not necessarily available when we are in business continuity mode.

→ *A One-Size-Fits-All Proposition.* The size of the organization, the complexity of its operations, whether you deliver a product or a service, whether you have central or dispersed operations, the number and location of facilities, the hazards and potential disasters faced by the company, the government regulations that must be met . . . these and a multitude of other variables make it essential that the development and implementation of a business continuity program be tailored to meet the needs and requirements of the organization.

→ *Insurance.* While insurance may be a viable option to replace tangibles—such as buildings, equipment, supplies, inventories, and even lost income—insurance cannot replace vital intangibles, which are things that are both even more difficult if not impossible to replace and are key to business survival. Customer confidence and trust, value of the name brand, and a positive image and reputation cannot be covered by insurance. Nor can insurance replace customers that may be lost due to an inability to fulfill contracts or meet delivery dates or terms of a service level agreement (SLA) when disaster strikes. (A service level agreement is a legally binding contract or formal agreement between a supplier and a customer that details the nature, quality, and scope of the service or product to be provided.)

→ *A Luxury.* Once considered a nice-to-have or when-we-get-around-to-it program, business continuity is now a fundamental core business practice, a necessity.

The Value of Business Continuity Planning

There is an often cited statistic regarding the success of businesses that have experienced a major disaster that has become a business continuity/disaster recovery version of an urban legend. The statistic has been used and quoted so widely and so often that few know its origin. The gist of this statistic—

which, incidentally, is from 2002 and from the U.S. Bureau of Labor Statistics—is that 43 percent of businesses never reopen and another 29 percent are no longer in business within two years of their experiencing a disaster. While out of context, this statistic is somewhat general and would seem to encompass everything from small mom-and-pop operations to large international corporate behemoths, it is nevertheless often used as a business continuity selling point.

History has proved that there are no companies that are so big and powerful that nothing bad can happen to them. Yet when there is no direct return on investment, it can be challenging to define the value of *business continuity planning*, which is the process to develop, implement, and maintain strategies and procedures to ensure that key operations and essential business functions can continue or quickly be restored in the event of a disaster, major emergency, or significant threat to the organization and its operations. Though not visible on a P&L statement, here are just a few examples of the value of business continuity that cannot be tied directly to the bottom line:

→ Customers are increasingly adding business continuity capability as a factor in the procurement selection process.

→ Rest assured that it is almost a certainty that some if not all of your competitors are using the fact that they have a comprehensive business continuity program as part of their marketing approach, especially if they believe you don't have such a program.

→ For some organizations, business continuity may be necessary in order to meet regulatory requirements. This is most notably true for banks and other financial services providers that in any way, shape, or form handle or physically or electronically process other people's money, as well as for healthcare businesses and pharmaceutical companies.

→ In extreme situations, it just may be that the survival of your business, at least as you know it today, depends on the success of your business continuity program.

→ It is morally and ethically correct to have a business continuity program to protect the interests of employees, owners, stockholders, customers and clients, and all stakeholders, including the general public.

→ Here is an undeniable truth: Customers expect products and services to be available and delivered as agreed upon, and they expect that you will meet your contractual obligations even when disasters occur. Developing and implementing a business continuity program is the vehicle for meeting those expectations.

→ See the preceding paragraph. In other words, developing, implementing, and maintaining a comprehensive business continuity program enables your organization to have continued operations in the face of disaster, thereby avoiding damage to the company and brand name image, thereby avoiding a loss of market share, thereby protecting the bottom line, thereby retaining corporate net worth, thereby helping to ensure the continuation of the business, and thus leading to continued employment. Enough said!

The bottom line is that in addition to being good business management, business continuity simply makes good sense.

A Historical Perspective

It may be helpful for those newly assigned to business continuity planning responsibilities, as well as for those more experienced in this regard, to take a look back at its history. Also interspersed as road markers in the discussion that follows are a few milestones in the evolution of supply chain management. (These "road markers" are presented here in italic type.)

The roots of business disaster management began with emergency preparedness and response planning required to comply with occupational safety standards enacted after the death of 146 workers in the 1911 Triangle Shirtwaist Factory fire in New York City. These efforts focused on preparations for actions to be taken to respond to what were primarily physical events, such as a fire, hurricane, or earthquake. Emergency response plans to address threats to the safety of people were already in place in many organizations, with a focus on life safety systems, emergency supplies and equipment, and trained employee emergency response teams. The primary goal was to keep people safe and protect the physical assets of the company and to begin stabilizing the company immediately following a disaster.

▷ ▷ ▷ ▷ ▷

In the first half of the twentieth century, the supply chain was a series of linear paper-based processes that connected suppliers, wholesalers, retailers, and end consumers—literally a chain of people and paper links. For most companies, the supply chain was limited in geographical scope and included a small number of suppliers and service providers. In the post–World War II economic boom, it became evident that there was a need to improve the existing low- or no-tech, nonscientific approach that was currently in place with methods and processes that better met current needs.

▷ ▷ ▷ ▷ ▷

Beginning in the late 1950s and into the 1960s and 1970s, companies increasingly recognized the need to protect and keep operational new and progressively more important technology, such as electronic data systems, networks, and advanced communications systems. During the second half of the 1970s, the term *disaster recovery* was first used to describe strategies and plans developed to restore IT, telecommunications, and other related technology. In some industries (for example, financial institutions), rigorous approaches and programs were implemented to meet increasingly strict regulatory requirements for the protection of critical systems and data. In other industries, backing up data on floppy disks and storing those disks in a desk drawer near the computer was considered disaster recovery.

▷ ▷ ▷ ▷ ▷

Beginning in the 1960s, management of the supply chain also benefited from newly developed approaches that combined information technology and business processes. Chief among the new management tools were software systems to manage inventory and maintain the appropriate level of stock in a warehouse. Identifying inventory requirements, setting targets, providing replenishment options, tracking item usage, reconciling inventory balances, and reporting up-to-date inventory status resulted in greater efficiency and profitability. In the 1970s, supply chain management **(SCM)** *became the commonly used terminology for this more advantageous approach.*

The 1960s and 1970s saw tremendous growth in international trade. This trend was motivated and supported by several factors. Geographic accessibility was being expanded while trade barriers were being removed. More international air cargo shipping locations and carriers led to increased air freight cost competitiveness. Standardized modular freight containers streamlined conveying freight among railroads, trucking companies, and cargo ships. Rapidly growing high-tech corporations were looking for new market opportunities and new production sites. Operations were moved to developing countries where manufacturers found lower production costs and a vast pool of low-cost unskilled labor. A result of expanded international trade was a supply chain that was more complex and more demanding than ever before.

▷ ▷ ▷ ▷ ▷

In the late 1970s, as the escalation of computerization and automated processes continued, a rapidly growing number of companies realized the critical need for the soon-to-be ubiquitous technology. Strategies were formulated to protect computerized data and systems, including redundant systems, off-site storage of data backups, and developing more sophisticated plans that provided guidance for the restoration of the organization's technology in the event of a disaster. It was just coincidental that some of the technology to be recovered was also needed to support business operations.

Disaster recovery planning continued to expand as the 1970s came to a close, creating a market for the growing number of contracted alternate sites that were being established throughout the United States and beyond. These sites were used for relocating and reconstituting IT operations when a data center was destroyed, severely damaged, nonoperational for whatever reason, or inaccessible. The backup computer centers, termed *hot sites*, provided alternate pre-equipped locations at which data center operations could be reestablished following a disaster. Hot sites became an increasingly used disaster recovery solution for data-dependent companies, in particular those with large, centralized mainframe computers, and a new industry was born. SunGard Recovery Services, Comdisco, and IBM were among the company names that first became synonymous with this new service industry.

▷ ▷ ▷ ▷ ▷

It was in the 1980s that the terms supply chain *and* supply chain management *were first used. While there is no documentation as to who originated the term* supply chain, *credit for coining the term* supply chain management *is given to consultant Keith Oliver of Booz Allen Hamilton, a strategy consulting firm that used the term when conducting a 1982 study to assess strategic approaches to managing the handling of raw goods and materials and product delivery.*

Also in the 1980s, supply chain management began to benefit from computerized systems used for managing many of the links in the supply chain. The new technology and faster delivery times to meet intense global competition were largely responsible for the adoption of inventory management techniques such as just-in-time (JIT), *a methodology that creates the movement of material into a specified location at a specified time, usually just before the material is needed in a manufacturing process;* Material Requirements Planning (MRP I), *a computer-based management tool that provides a manufacturer with a means of determining what products to produce and in what quantities based on the response to what the manufacturer sells to its customers; and the expanded* Manufacturing Resource Planning (MRP II), *which includes added functions throughout the organization, such as marketing and finance.*

It was in the early 1990s that companies began broadening their supply chain view beyond manufacturing facilities to an enterprise-wide approach, called enterprise resource planning (ERP)—*an integrated information system that serves all departments within an enterprise to facilitate coordination of manufacturing processes with enterprise-wide back-end processes. This was followed by the realization that to fully succeed in making certain that all available company resources were managed and used effectively required looking outside the company and including the highly interdependent supply chain.*

▷ ▷ ▷ ▷ ▷

The mid-1990s brought the growing realization that disaster recovery, which involved recovering only the organization's technology, would not necessarily result in the organization being able to deliver its product or service in the wake of a disaster. An "aha" moment occurred. To be successful in recovering from the impacts of a disaster and maintaining an acceptable level of profitability, the critical business processes of each unit of the organization must be considered in the disaster planning process and be involved in the development and implementation of recovery strategies. With this realization, many organizations expanded their disaster planning to include recovery of enterprise-wide critical work processes—the business of the business—rather than just the supporting technology.

With the addition of recovery of business operations to the disaster planning process, seventy-two hours, several days, a week, or even longer were considered acceptable—even admirable—times in which to restore business operations and the necessary data center support. For the majority of organizations that were expanding from a strictly disaster recovery approach to a more inclusive business recovery approach, the assumption was that since IT had done such a great job with disaster recovery, it was only right that IT also own business recovery. Almost overnight, IT professionals found themselves becoming business recovery planners.

Proactive disaster recovery and business recovery planning was still a developing business practice, however. Over the years, the scope had broadened in part as a result of the continuing efforts of first, disaster recovery planners, and later, business recovery planners, to raise awareness of the need to protect not just technology or ensure the safety of the organization's physical plant, but also to sustain operations. Yet, during an audit, while check-the-box questions may have been asked about the existence of a disaster recovery plan or even a business recovery plan, it was uncommon for an auditor to conduct a full review of the planning process, plan document content, and test and update records.

To think back to the mid-1990s when disaster planning first began addressing operational recovery—not at all that long ago—and consider what transpired before and after that time is pretty amazing. The corporate world's view of the need to prepare for and respond to disasters had seen significant progress from an "it won't happen here" or a "we'll deal with it if it happens" approach to understanding the need to proactively manage risks.

In 1999, Y2K was a serious concern throughout the modern world. Businesses and government agencies became more aware of the significance of business recovery and disaster recovery planning, and they dedicated significant resources to addressing the looming threat of a worldwide failure of computer systems. Planning for Y2K was significant in that it was the first time that external threats were taken into account. Essential suppliers, shippers, and even utility providers and communications companies were identified and questioned about their level of preparedness.

Midnight on December 31, 1999, passed with almost no fallout, and Y2K became a nonevent. Was it never a threat? Did the extensive planning and mitigation that took place prevent a catastrophe? While we can never really know what the outcome would have been had nothing been done, I side with those who say that a major disaster was prevented by the proactive approach taken to identify, mitigate, and manage the threat.

▷ ▷ ▷ ▷ ▷

The period from 1980 through 1999 saw dramatic changes in the very nature of supply chain operation. Distributed networked environments with multitiered processes increasingly became the norm. Changes came at a continually more rapid pace in ongoing efforts to meet escalating customer demands. Supply chains capable of quickly recognizing and responding to the global economy's requirements for quality output became the expectation.

As business moved into the new millennium, outsourcing became the commonly accepted norm in supply chain operations, from the procurement of materials and parts to services that were previously internal. Warehousing, inventory control, and transportation were frequently subcontracted to outside companies. As a result, supply chain executives became responsible for managing multiple resources well beyond their organization's four walls.

▷ ▷ ▷ ▷ ▷

With the dawning of a new millennium, seemingly ever present disasters, old and new, continued to heighten the awareness of the need for business to proactively manage risks. Business requirements became more demanding and even more rapidly paced, resulting in a growing awareness that for many organizations, restoring operations in a week or two or in even a few days was no longer acceptable. The need was to continue operations, not recover them. The new challenge was to plan for business continuity—the immediate or rapid restoration of the delivery of the organization's service or product following any disaster.

To accomplish this after many years of a very internal-centric approach to business continuity planning, there is a growing awareness that we must plan for disasters that occur within and outside our own organizations. It is now necessary to consider threats to businesses and organizations that play a critical role in our operations, even those well beyond national borders and in locations as distant and diverse as Bulgaria, China, and Taiwan. In today's business world, developing effective business continuity capability requires full consideration of suppliers, contractors, utility providers, financial institutions, business partners, all other elements of our supply chain, government agencies, and even our customers.

Now more than ever before, the reality is that the supply chain is susceptible to potentially crippling disaster-caused disruptions, and supply chain continuity must be fully integrated in a comprehensive enterprise-wide business continuity program. When we rely on another company to sustain our operations, any disruption in its operations is a potential disruption or even a disaster for us.

With this growing realization comes heightened customer awareness that a supplier's lack of a mature, tested business continuity plan could disrupt its operations as well. This has led to an increasing trend toward questioning suppliers, service providers, and contractors about their business continuity capabilities. In some cases, proof is requested in the form of an audit report or review of a business continuity plan together with its review, training, and testing history. I urge my clients to take this approach, and at the same time I caution them to expect that their customers will request the same of them.

While already an established business practice, the growth of business continuity planning after the previously unimaginable events of September 11, 2001, was explosive and rapid. In the weeks and months that followed, businesses witnessed and experienced significant differences between those that had developed operational resilience as a result of having mature, tested business continuity programs and those that would suffer tremendous setbacks or in some cases not survive as a result of not having developed business continuity capabilities. The hard-learned lessons were many, and they have resulted in improvements in business continuity planning that fully includes critical business functions well beyond the data center. Business continuity is now even more widely accepted throughout the corporate world and among government agencies as a business management issue.

Another consequence of 9/11 was the seemingly sudden appearance of a multitude of new business continuity–related businesses or divisions of existing businesses. Dubbed "Nine-Twelve Companies" by the late John Laye, a longtime emergency management and business continuity practitioner, these companies provide everything from emergency supplies to relocation services, from evacuation training to software and outsourcing for developing and maintaining disaster recovery and business continuity programs, and from emergency notification systems to building restoration services. Where there is a need, or a perceived need, new companies continue to emerge to fill the void created by a perceived or real need.

A recent example of new terminology—a phrase du jour, if you will—now adopted for frequent usage is *resilient organization*. Frequently used in a multitude of ways by different people and groups, but not always well, the word *resilient* is now applied across many business and academic disciplines and in numerous different contexts. It has also become a favorite among those in the supply chain profession. There is little actual universal consensus regarding what resilience is, what it means, and perhaps most importantly, how any organization or business unit within the organization might reach greater resilience and thus earn the designation of resilient organization.

Is a resilient organization one that is capable of functioning at the highest levels in all aspects of its operation and continuing to meet its goals come what may? Is it a company or any type of organization whose operations and employees are flexible and prepared to manage disruptions? Is a resilient organization one that is able to achieve its mission in spite of any type of large or small disaster? If the response to any of these questions is *yes*, then having a business continuity program would seem to be a prerequisite for any organization seeking the right to identify itself as a resilient organization.

Supply chain business continuity and risk management have and will continue to become increasingly important. This trend has been reinforced as a result of what was experienced following disaster events like Hurricane Katrina in 2005, when it was again shown that companies that had incorporated the supply chain in their business continuity planning were able to recover successfully. Supply chain managers in these organizations were directly involved in the business continuity planning and testing. As a result, they were able to quickly respond and make the right decisions to sustain or restore supply chain operations.

Over the years, the focus of disaster recovery—business recovery—and business continuity has matured and grown to meet the needs of a rapidly changing business environment. While professionals originally focused on reconstituting the IT environment after a disaster occurred, we now look for ways to avoid and mitigate risks and to maintain or restore operations throughout the organization. While today's global markets and supply chains, as well as national and international mergers, bring great opportunities, these opportunities are accompanied by embedded risks. The world is an increasingly risky place in which to conduct business, and the risks can no longer be defined within company or national boundaries. It is more important than ever that a comprehensive approach to business continuity planning embraces all interdependencies both inside and outside the company, including business partners, suppliers, and contractors, regardless of where they are located.

Business Continuity Planning: A New Responsibility

In the 1990s, it was not at all unusual when speaking with company employees to hear that they had just learned that part of their job responsibilities—perhaps buried somewhere in the human resources job description—included business recovery team member, department business recovery representative, or division disaster recovery liaison. For other employees, disaster-related responsibilities simply fell under the "other duties as assigned" category.

If the employees tried to get additional information, they may have been told, "Don't worry about it unless someone calls you to attend a planning meeting," or, "There's actually nothing to do," or perhaps, "There's a copy of the plan somewhere in your office that someone wrote a couple of years ago. Take a look at it when you get a chance."

The employees had just joined the ranks of the overlooked, misunderstood, neglected, and in worst-case situations abused individuals charged with dealing with threats to the well-being of the organization and its employees. As a rule, this new designation of business recovery team member (or whatever it was called) was seldom accompanied by additional resources or a lightened workload in primary responsibilities to compensate for the newly acquired responsibilities. In addition, the accompanying time frame in which the newly assigned projects were to be completed was often unrealistic.

Many employees weren't even aware that the organization had a business recovery or disaster recovery program, let alone understood its purpose or how it related to them, their department, or the company at large. While executives and senior managers may have known that disaster recovery and business recovery existed within the organization, there may not have been a full understanding of what it entailed or what was required to develop and maintain a viable business recovery program.

Business continuity is still often considered the "new kid on the block" in business and government. Those involved in these disciplines, directly and indirectly, are in a unique position in that they are engaged in a relatively new and growing profession and business practice. Business continuity planning is challenging, interesting, and rewarding. There is something very fulfilling in knowing what a tremendous contribution your role in it is making to your organization. It is also a learning opportunity, a chance to know more about the organization and its operations well beyond the borders of your own department or business unit.

Today, the way in which companies and organizations view the need to manage severe emergencies and disasters has both changed and stayed the same. For some organizations, it is now unacceptable for the most time-critical functions to be non-operational for minutes, if not seconds. Yet even today, it can still be a challenge to sell business continuity to the powers that be within an organization and to gain not just agreement that it is beneficial but true executive commitment to the business continuity program. This is particularly true when the economy takes a downturn and other initiatives and programs are viewed as having greater importance.

Some companies are still not sure where business continuity belongs on the org chart. Is it part of IT? Should it be part of operations, or finance, or security? Do we need a new, separate department or business unit? For now, there is not a single response to these questions, and the answers vary from organization to organization.

Perhaps the greatest challenge is the ongoing need to make business continuity an integral part of the organization and its culture rather than the unwanted outsider.

As business continuity further matures, we continue to search for improvements. In spite of ongoing growing pains, business continuity planning continues its evolution to becoming the central core of integrated risk management. There is growing realization and understanding that managing an organization's risks is no longer the responsibility of the person who manages the insurance program, the financial manager, the head of security, or the auditors. A best practices approach to managing risk requires an integrated, coordinated, enterprise-wide approach. To be successful, a business continuity program must incorporate each of the company's units. This requires a planning approach that includes the entire supply chain, and to do that well, all of the organization's supply chain professionals must be involved.

At one time or another, when we were kids sitting in the backseat of the car on a family trip, each of us likely asked, probably more than once, "Are we there yet?" Today, if you asked me this question about business continuity, I would acknowledge that I'm not sure how much further we have to travel, but I would respond with a resounding, "No, but we're getting there."

In attempting to be of assistance to those who are involved in supply chain business continuity or who want or need to know more about business continuity planning for any reason, this book attempts to walk a tightrope. That is, it tries to take a somewhat complex and relatively new component of managing organizational risk—business continuity planning—and keep the content clear-cut and understandable while providing the necessary depth and insights into the concepts. And all the while, the main and most basic goal is to provide guidance for those with new or continuing responsibility for applying those concepts to an increasingly complicated supply chain.

Some Additional Key Terms

As with most disciplines, lines of work, and subject matter, the vocabulary of business continuity and related terminology has been coined, has developed, and has evolved over the years. There are ongoing attempts to establish a universal lexicon that have resulted in less than full acceptance. And, as with every facet of our culture, those practicing business continuity planning love to talk in acronym-ese: BCP, BIA, DR, DRP, EM, ERM, RTO, or—as I like to think of it—"business continuity alphabet soup." In addition to terms specific to business continuity, here are some of the generally accepted terms and acronyms used in this book:

→ *Disaster:* A destructive or disruptive event, usually sudden, beyond the response capabilities of the organization where it has occurred. Typically brings great damage, loss, or destruction. For businesses, any event that causes a cessation of vital business functions; an event requiring immediate action to ensure the continuation or resumption of operations.

→ *Emergency Management:* A process within a comprehensive risk management program that includes all the components of the overall approach to managing major emergencies and disasters by addressing risks to people, facilities, equipment, and operations.

→ *Disaster Recovery:* The restoration of an organization's technology to provide the IT, telecommunications, and related technology needed to support business continuity objectives.

→ *Disaster Recovery Plan (DRP):* Documented strategies and detailed procedures for the recovery of computing and network hardware and software and electronic data.

→ *Enterprise Risk Management (ERM):* Terminology increasingly used by risk management and business continuity practitioners. The identification and treatment of risks encompassing all aspects of the business or organization with the goal of identifying, measuring, managing, and minimizing risks. Planning, organizing, leading, and controlling the activities of an organization to minimize the effects of all risks.

An expanded list of selected business continuity and supply chain terminology and acronyms used in this book is found in the Glossary. These definitions were written and edited from my perspective and reflect their usage in this book. *Note:* As there is not yet total agreement on the definitions and usage of these words and terms, it is almost certain that you have heard and read and/or will hear and read definitions that are different from those provided. I respect and appreciate the differences, which I believe are primarily a reflection of a still maturing business practice. The concepts and best practices and their application are the same.

There are differences in terminology among different types of businesses, between government and nongovernment organizations, from one geographic area to another, and even among business units within organizations. Of great importance is the need to standardize usage of the agreed-upon terms throughout an enterprise, to develop a business continuity glossary, and to take the steps necessary to ensure that the terminology is used and understood throughout the organization and by key stakeholders.

Going Forward

In spite of ongoing efforts to adopt universally accepted business continuity terminology, there are many inconsistencies in their usage. For example, business continuity and disaster recovery, two terms with very different meanings, are often used interchangeably, leading to misconceptions. The use of business continuity acronyms known only to those directly involved in the business continuity planning process can also get in the way of shared understanding.

The importance of consistently using fully understood terms throughout an organization cannot be overstated. Having a common language with standard terminology provides a basis for understanding, developing, and implementing a successful enterprise-wide business continuity program.

→ Check to see if there is an accepted lexicon of business continuity terms used consistently throughout your organization.

→ Review currently used terminology to determine if it accurately reflects business continuity best practices.

→ Take steps to develop or have developed a common lexicon or to make necessary revisions in existing terminology.

→ Spell out and define all business continuity acronyms.

→ Have business continuity terminology officially adopted for use across the organization.

→ Include the lexicon as a glossary in all business continuity plans and related documents.

CHAPTER *2*

The Business Continuity Program: Who Owns It, What Drives It?

BUSINESS'S ABILITY to continue operations following a disaster is directly related to the degree of its business continuity planning prior to the disaster and the quality of the resulting business continuity program. Critical to the long-term success of such a program is having responsibility for business continuity properly placed in the organizational structure. This includes an executive sponsor for the program who not only has authority and visibility throughout the company but who also understands risk management as it relates to the organization, its mission, and its strategic direction. It also includes the individual who oversees and has primary responsibility for the business continuity planning process and the person who then has ongoing ownership of the program.

In a very true sense, every business unit and every employee in the organization is responsible for the ongoing welfare of the organization, even though they may not be decision makers or have direct, specific business continuity planning responsibilities. This also includes everyone who is a part of the organization's supply chain business units.

Business continuity planning is an initiative that many organizations have undertaken independently, each for their own set of reasons. Other organizations have been encouraged or required to address business continuity by influences outside the organization. Identifying and understanding the business continuity drivers at the onset of the planning project is important in establishing the goals for the process and its outcome. Equally important is the need to periodically revisit the original drivers to determine if new or revised requirements have created a need to revise or enhance the organization's business continuity approach and strategies.

Managing Risk

As a basic principle, the board of directors or the highest executive level of an organization has ultimate responsibility for ensuring that the organization is prepared to manage risk and when necessary recover from a disaster.

Executives and high-level managers all manage risk. The chair or chief executive officer (CEO) manages the organization's reputational risks. The chief financial officer (CFO) is responsible for managing the organization's financial risks. The chief operating officer (COO) deals with operational risks, while the chief information officer (CIO) is responsible for the organization's data center and IT infrastructure risks. Risks from internal and external attacks are largely the concern of the chief security officer (CSO).

Astute board members and executives realize that in today's increasingly risk-adverse business climate, business continuity planning is an essential element of an overall risk management approach that improves operational reliability, quality, and even efficiency, and thus the bottom line. Where there may be a disconnect is somewhere between the time executives agree that business continuity planning is needed and the time they truly commit to it by personally and fiscally supporting the program and providing the necessary resources.

Executives are continually and understandably concerned about cost justification and return on investment (ROI).

Any and all expenditures—whether in the form of cash and/or time or people resources—are always a consideration. The recession that struck in the late 2000s and its challenges have only exacerbated the need for prudent fiscal controls. Showing a traditional direct ROI from a business continuity program can be challenging, as many of the returns are not tangible and do not appear on a profit and loss statement.

Demonstrating the full value of the investment in business continuity planning requires the inclusion of not just the benefits of the program's chief purpose, which is to manage the risks and disasters that we hope will never occur. It also requires that the day-to-day benefits from the program be rolled into the cost/benefit equation. This may demonstrate that business continuity helps pay for itself well beyond the management of disasters and near disasters.

A *business impact analysis* (BIA) is conducted during the planning process and includes a full examination and documentation of procedures and processes. The primary purpose of the BIA is to analyze all operations with a goal of identifying and documenting the functions throughout the organization that are most critical to the organization's mission. For each of these critical functions, the internal and external dependencies, required staffing, IT support, special equipment, and restoration time objective are identified. The results of this in-depth analysis often include identification of opportunities for day-to-day improvements, better use of shared resources, and even the possible elimination of duplicate resource costs. The identification of departmental interdependencies helps foster relationships between business units, particularly in organizations in which departments and other business units tend to function as silos. Identifying single points of failure that were previously unnoticed or unheeded may prevent future disasters. Cross-training to help ensure post-disaster critical staffing develops more knowledgeable, better qualified employees and allows distribution of tasks as needed on a day-to-day basis. For some organizations, the resulting BIA report also includes information that provides a greater depth of understanding of the organization and how it functions than was ever collectively available before.

From the IT side of the house, establishing the priority order and time frame in which to restore critical systems, applications, processes, etc., is helpful when the small non-disaster data center failures occur as well as in the event of a disaster-caused outage. Identification of potential IT service interruptions during the hazard assessment phase and mitigating these threats with monitoring and tracking tools and procedures can lead to problems being corrected before a system failure creates a disaster.

Today's supply chain executives and professionals do have responsibility for managing risk. With globalization, worldwide supply chains, and concerns about product safety, supplier risks can threaten an organization's reputation, security, brand name, and ability to continue operations. While supply chain professionals are not typically assigned primary responsibility for an organization's overall business continuity program, the success or failure of the company's strategies to continue or resume operations following a disaster likely depends on the supply chain operating at an acceptable level. A failed link in the supply chain can be the disaster or can prevent the organization from restoring operations following a disaster. Whether business continuity responsibilities are well detailed in your job description or simply included in the "other duties as assigned" category, everyone who carries out supply chain business functions also has some level of responsibility for managing risk. Everyone, therefore, has a business continuity role.

Who's in Charge, Who's Responsible?

Every day, all employees, including executives, juggle ongoing responsibilities, special projects, and emergencies that require their time, attention, and resources. This can result in a tendency to delay or ignore tasks and assignments that are not directly and specifically delegated, spelled out, or considered to be a priority. Having no assigned ownership and responsibility for business continuity may result in it being on the "when I have more time" list or the "it's not my job, let someone else do it" list. This is a critical mistake.

Ensuring that business continuity is given the necessary focus begins with one executive taking ownership and assigning qualified people. Without the appropriate organizational structure and the right people assigned to business continuity— beginning with the planning process and then on a permanent sustained basis—the program will quickly begin to deteriorate and ultimately fall apart even if the initial planning process is highly successful.

As previously stated, business continuity is still a relatively new business discipline that has not yet found a permanent home on a traditional organization chart. Disaster recovery— the restoration of the data center and related technology—was founded in the IT department and still resides there. In many organizations, when programs were expanded to include business continuity, IT retained responsibility and ownership. Even today, in a great many businesses and organizations, the expense of business continuity as well as disaster recovery is included in the IT budget. Further, particularly in small to midsize businesses, it is not unusual to see an IT executive or manager in charge of the business continuity program.

With executive leadership more accountable and personally responsible than ever before for protecting the interests of the businesses they lead, there is growing agreement that ultimate responsibility for business continuity lies with the highest levels of the organization—the C-suite and the board of directors. Members of the board have responsibility for protecting the organization's assets and safeguarding the organization's survival. While at a minimum the board should review the business continuity program annually, that does not always happen. In some organizations, the highest levels of management may have only a rudimentary understanding of the requirements and benefits of a comprehensive program. In some extreme cases, the board and senior executives may not even know whether such a program exists in their organization.

An increasing number of organizations now have a full-time business continuity planning manager and/or a business continuity planning group. In the 2008 *Continuity Insights/ KPMG Business Continuity Management Benchmarking Survey* of private sector, public sector, and not-for-profit enterprises, approximately 25 percent of respondents identified the business continuity program coordinator as a director, manager, or VP of business continuity management. In the future, as business continuity planning continues to evolve and mature and is recognized as a core business function, it may not be unusual to see large organizations add a board-level executive, called the chief continuity officer (CCO), to oversee business continuity. For now, the list of job titles of those who have responsibility for it is long and all over the chart as efforts continue to build consensus about where responsibility and ownership best fit.

A very slowly building trend in recent years, particularly in larger corporations, is to combine business continuity, disaster recovery, security, risk management/insurance, safety, and other related business units to form one department. The head of this department reports to an upper-level executive, such as the organization's CEO, COO, or CFO. While it may at first seem that there is no direct relationship among these functions, the underlying responsibility of each of these business units is the continued well-being and safety of the organization and its employees, facilities, and operations. This combined management approach helps avoid both gaps and duplication of effort.

A business continuity program will succeed only when all elements of the supply chain, beginning with supply chain executives and managers and including all the employees who keep the supply chain functioning smoothly, are included in a comprehensive approach to business continuity planning.

What Drives the Need for a Business Continuity Program?

There are numerous reasons for initiating a business continuity planning project, and what persuades each decision maker to support and finance the initiative can be unpredictable and may even seem subjective. Here's one view of what it takes to sell business continuity: seeing smoke billowing from the building next to your company's headquarters. Watching flames coming from that building may result in agreement that business continuity planning is necessary. Seeing a "Closed" sign in front of the rubble of the burned-out building on a daily basis will likely foster a true understanding of the need for and an accompanying commitment to the development and implementation of a comprehensive business continuity program.

Realistically, robust business continuity planning may have multiple drivers. Some come from within the organization, based on managers realizing the need for planning to respond to higher levels of risk that have increased the organization's operational vulnerability. The requirement for a business continuity program might also come from the executive level, perhaps in the form of an organizational policy to ensure the safety of employees and continued service to customers. Still others within the organization may see the development and implementation of a business continuity program as an ethical or moral issue, protecting the interests and well-being of the organization and its employees, owners, the local economy, and all other stakeholders.

In other organizations, the drivers might come from external businesses, organizations, or agencies—such as insurance companies and regulatory agencies—that have a vested interest in your level of business continuity capability. The primary project driver may even be a request from a customer who wants your organization to demonstrate that you have the capability of delivering your product or service should you experience a disaster.

Increasingly, business continuity has become a marketing issue. The heart of business continuity planning is development of the capability to deliver your product or service—all the time, and with no exceptions. Today, beyond price and quality considerations, potential customers want to know that you have plans in place to meet their needs and requirements and to fulfill contracts and service level agreements even when events threaten your continued operations. Such prospective customers may well ask about your company's business continuity program. In addition, there is every likelihood that competitors are using their capability to continue operations following a disaster as a marketing advantage. That capability may become the deciding factor for a prospective customer when a final selection is made.

Even attempting to gain new business through a competitive bidding process may involve having a business continuity program in place. Some businesses and government agencies require that a company have a validated business continuity plan in place to be eligible to submit a proposal or bid. For example, under the Federal Acquisition Regulations (FAR)—the rules issued by agencies of the federal government to oversee the acquisition process by which government agencies purchase goods and services—the ability to perform during a disaster may be a bidding requirement for some solicitations for products and services.

The motivation for developing and maintaining a business continuity program may also be a financial one. What would one hour of disaster-caused downtime cost your organization? A day? A week? A month? Longer? Simply doing the math may present one of the best possible incentives for developing a business continuity program.

There may also be legal reasons to incorporate business continuity planning into the corporate culture. While I am not an attorney or qualified to give legal advice, here is a simple way to determine if there may be legal requirements for a business continuity program and whether there may be potential liability if an organization does not prepare to respond to and recover from disasters. Business liability is, in part, judged on the basis of:

→ What a "reasonable person" would do given the probability that a disaster could occur

→ Whether the risk was known or should have been known

→ The magnitude of resulting harm and the effort required to institute proper precautions

Based on the types, number, and scope of disasters that have occurred over the past several years, it would seem difficult for any organization to claim that it had no knowledge of the risk potential or the resulting impact on the organization's ability to fulfill its business obligations should a disaster occur.

For some organizations, the earliest impetus for the development of a business continuity program may have been an audit requirement. Both internal and external auditors are now taking greater interest in business continuity. Both internal and external audits are important to businesses and are required for organizations that are publicly traded, are financial institutions, or are part of healthcare and related industries, as well as for government agencies. In the past, an auditor may have asked whether an organization had a business continuity plan and then checked off a box according to the response. Today, a business continuity audit check may consist of reviewing the plan and perhaps the record of updates and tests, as well as interviews with selected key employees and stakeholders. Other audits are much more complex and stringent and may involve an audit team that reviews and analyzes almost every aspect of the business continuity program. This may include a full analysis of the business continuity planning process, a review of business continuity–related contracts, an examination of business continuity training and testing, and a thorough review to determine how inclusive the plan is, whether it adheres to current best practices, when it was last updated, and when it was last tested. More in-depth audits, such as those required by regulatory agencies, may check the plan and the overall program against a lengthy list of requirements and standards.

Various standards and regulations look closely at business continuity capability. For example, there are a number of relevant requirements from the International Organization for Standardization (ISO). (The ISO is a network of the national standards institutes of approximately 160 countries that provides standards and guidelines for quality in the manufacturing and service industries.)

For many types of businesses and organizations, there are increasingly stringent regulatory requirements for business continuity and/or disaster recovery programs. Again, this primarily includes financial institutions, health organizations, and pharmaceutical companies.

In the United States, a small sampling of the federal bureaus and regulatory agencies to which a company may be required to submit regular reports includes the following:

→ Consumer Product Safety Commission

→ Environmental Protection Agency (EPA)

→ Federal Deposit Insurance Corporation (FDIC)

→ Federal Trade Commission (FTC)

→ Food and Drug Administration (FDA)

→ Joint Commission on Accreditation of Healthcare Organizations (JCAHO)

→ Occupational Safety and Health Administration (OSHA)

→ U.S. Customs and Border Protection

→ U.S. Fish and Wildlife Service

It is likely that based on your industry, you can identify other federal regulatory agencies, as well as state and local bureaus and agencies, to which you must respond and report or with whom you work on an ongoing basis.

As an example, regulations and permits require that a chemical company must comply with the regulations of several agencies if it discharges to local waterways and has stack emissions. Just some of the required filings and reporting include monthly discharge monitoring reports; annual emergency planning and community right-to-know act emissions reports; spill prevention, control, and countermeasures reports; benzene waste water reports; fugitive and point source emission reporting for benzene; air compliance reports; quantifying amounts of annual hazardous waste reports; annual financial assurance reporting; and waste minimization reports.

Noncompliance can result in significant fines, sanctions, and harm to the company's reputation. In extreme cases, it can lead to the loss of licenses and permits and a forced shutdown of operations. In most cases, requirements for regulatory compliance and reporting continue with little or no latitude following a disaster.

Chapter 10 includes a detailed discussion of these and other business continuity standards and regulations.

Business Continuity and Risk Management: Similarities and Differences

As a result of the ongoing evolution of business continuity and risk management, it is not surprising that questions are raised about the relationship between the two. Where does risk management fit in this picture? Is business continuity part of risk management or vice versa? Are they parallel functions? Do they intersect? Do they overlap? An easy response to all these questions would be that it depends on whether you ask the risk manager or the business continuity manager. However, there are no simple answers. Much depends on the business, how the organization approaches managing its risks, and the responsibilities assigned to risk management and to business continuity.

There are many definitions of risk management, with the result that the term is used differently by different people and among different organizations. Here is one simple definition: policies, procedures, and practices involved in identification, analysis, assessment, control, and avoidance, minimization, or elimination of unacceptable risks. As risk is always inherent in business, some risk managers may expand on this definition with an explanation that risk management is not the avoidance of risk. Rather, it is the management of all risks throughout the organization to lessen negative effects to an acceptable level and take advantage of any opportunities that risks may present.

The role and responsibilities of a risk manager are a reflection of a profession where job descriptions have changed over the years and may vary greatly among organizations. Responsibilities may include managing an organization's insurance program and making recommendations regarding coverage, administering the insurance program, and selection of and negotiation with insurance carriers and brokers. Risk managers may also be responsible for safety programs; providing evaluations of potential risks and losses to financial institutions, accountants, and legal counsel; or evaluating risks associated with new projects, products, and initiatives. Today, as our definitions of risk and risk management continue to morph, it is increasingly common for the risk manager to head up the organization's more extensive enterprise risk management (ERM) program.

There are several similarities in traditional risk management and business continuity. For example, both:

→ Address uncertainties
→ Are proactive
→ Are systematic and structured processes
→ Must be customized and tailored to the organization in order to be effective
→ Must be dynamic, ongoing, and responsive to change
→ Must be continually improved and enhanced
→ Create value

There are some logical comparisons in the application of risk management and business continuity processes, as shown in Figure 2-1.

Business continuity may have a solid or dotted line reporting responsibility to risk management, or the two may operate as autonomous silo functions. While both risk management and business continuity have as their core objective protection of the organization, perhaps the principal difference is their primary focus. While risk management has traditionally focused on risks related to financial markets, projects, and legal liabilities, as well as credit risks, the primary focus of business continuity is operational risks and risks to the related support systems. To more completely meet the needs of organizations with both risk management and business continuity functions, it is necessary to define the specific roles and responsibilities and reporting structure of both. This helps to avoid planning

FIGURE 2-1.

COMPARISON OF RISK MANAGEMENT AND BUSINESS CONTINUITY PROCESSES.

Risk Management	*Business Continuity*
Identification of risks and related opportunities; measurement and assessment of identified risks and the related exposure	*Hazard assessment/Risk analysis:* Identification of risks and their impact on operations; mitigation to lessen impact of disasters
Determination of target level of exposure (risk appetite)	*Business impact analysis (BIA):* Identification of mission-critical functions within the organization
Management plan that includes controls, actions, and fallbacks	*Business continuity plan:* Documentation of strategies, procedures, and action items

gaps, overlaps, and even turf wars and ensures the necessary coordination and integration.

Rules, Regulations, Requirements, Guidelines, and Implications

In the beginning, there were no hard and fast rules, no regulations, and few guidelines to assist in developing a business continuity program. Instead, there was trial and error resulting in a great deal of learning. It was a Nike approach: "Just do it." That has changed significantly and continues to change in both the corporate and government sectors. There are increasingly stringent regulatory requirements for business continuity programs that encompass disaster recovery requirements. This is particularly true for some types of businesses, such as financial institutions, publicly traded companies, health organizations, and pharmaceutical companies. Wading through the ever changing requirements can be a daunting task.

While not specific to business continuity or disaster recovery, the Gramm-Leach-Bliley Act of 1999, the Health Insurance Portability and Accountability Act (HIPAA) of 1996, the Sarbanes-Oxley Act of 2002, and the Six Sigma business management strategy all have business continuity or disaster recovery implications. More recently, business continuity has been directly tied to disaster recovery planning requirements in both the United States and Great Britain. In the United States, this occurred with the Voluntary Private Sector Preparedness Accreditation and Certification Program (PS-Prep), which is mandated by Title IX of the Implementing Recommendations of the 9/11 Commission Act, passed in 2007, an offshoot of the Homeland Security Act. In Britain, the British Standards Institution BS-25999 (also from 2007) outlines standards and guidelines for voluntary business continuity audit and certification. (See Chapter 10 for more information.)

A Business Continuity Plan vs. A Business Continuity Program

Unfortunately, it is not uncommon to hear, "We need to write a business continuity plan." Perhaps it is the requirement to have a document to show auditors or a customer or to have a deliverable to complete an assigned project that creates this be-all, end-all drive for THE PLAN.

In reality, a *business continuity program* is needed to effectively protect the organization from disasters. A *plan* is a document, printed copies of which are typically kept in a three-ring binder, that authenticates a program. A *program* is a dynamic, ongoing, comprehensive process. It is composed of several key components that encompass conducting a hazard assessment and implementing a hazard mitigation program, conducting a business impact analysis, developing business continuity strategies, conducting training and exercises, procuring needed supplies and equipment, and conducting regularly scheduled reviews and revisions—in addition to developing a printed plan that documents all elements of the program and gives specific guidance as to who will carry out the strategies when a disaster occurs.

Developing a plan is a project with an end; in contrast, a program is dynamic and has no conclusion. Writing, maintaining, and revising the plan is only one part of the program. Without an ongoing process to ensure that the business continuity program is reviewed, revised, and included in the change management process, it is highly likely that a plan document will become static. Without a comprehensive program, even the very best plan quickly diminishes in value over a relatively short time.

A program also includes specific actions to ensure that business continuity is embedded in the organization's culture and day-to-day operations. Communicating the program throughout the organization, sharing information, and providing awareness training for all employees are critical elements of a business continuity program. Bear in mind that if employees do not know that the organization has a business continuity program and are not aware of their role, however small it may be, the business continuity program does not exist for them.

Going Forward

Some companies have a highly visible business continuity program that is well communicated throughout the enterprise and is an integral part of the organization's culture. In other organizations, the program is a well-kept secret known only to those who are directly responsible for it and perhaps those to whom they report. In yet other organizations, there is a plan document that is distributed only to the individuals who are expected to carry out the actions outlined when a disaster occurs. To better understand the level of commitment given to business continuity in your company, learn more about where it is located within the organization and what drives the necessity for a program.

> → Find out who is the executive sponsor of your organization's business continuity program.
> → Learn who is in charge of the business continuity planning process and to whom they report.

→ Discover who has ongoing ownership of the business continuity program and to whom they report.

→ Ascertain what drives the need for a business continuity program in your organization.

→ Determine whether your organization has a business continuity program or only a business continuity plan document.

CHAPTER *3*

Business Continuity Best Practices

COMPANIES THAT ARE fully aware of business continuity have applied a best practice business continuity planning process to develop a mature program that both aligns with current standards and is tailored to address operational risks and meet the needs of the organization and its stakeholders.

Included in this chapter is one approach to current business continuity best practices. This approach reflects the latest iteration of the methodology I have successfully used over the past twenty years in working with a broad range of businesses and organizations. Over time, accepted best practices have changed to meet the evolving scope and requirements of business continuity planning, and they will continue to change as business continuity further matures as a business practice.

It is important to keep in mind that business continuity planning is neither a one-size-fits-all blueprint nor is it an all-or-nothing proposition. Instead, it is more of a spectrum of readiness. Requirements and standards vary among industries. Continuity strategies that work for one company can result in absolute failure for another. An event that is a disaster for one company can be an insignificant inconvenience for another. Following accepted business continuity best practices to the letter may not always be the best approach for every organization. Doing so may simply not be feasible for some companies because of time or money constraints or lack of full executive level commitment. Best practices are most effective when they are applied in combination with real-world common sense, intelligence, and innovation, while always keeping in mind the company's culture, situation, and requirements.

Developing a Business Continuity Program

While a plan is a necessity to codify and document the business continuity program as well as to provide guidance for implementing continuity strategies, a comprehensive program must go well beyond what to do after a disaster occurs. A business continuity program must incorporate these four components:

1. Hazard assessment and mitigation
2. Preparedness
3. Response
4. Recovery/continuity

Simply put, the plan is the operator's manual for the program, and as such it must both provide detailed procedures for carrying out continuity strategies and outline requirements for training, testing, and program maintenance.

A hazard assessment—the first component of the business continuity program—identifies and quantifies the threats and risks to a business in a specific location. Mitigation involves the planning and actions taken to eliminate those threats and risks to the extent possible prior to their occurrence. This could, for example, include installing electric power generators or arranging for leased generators before a power outage occurs. When the risks identified cannot be eliminated, mitigation involves the planning and actions taken in advance of a destructive or disruptive event in order to reduce, avoid, or protect against its impact—for instance, installing security systems and limiting building access to eliminate or control unauthorized access to facilities to avoid sabotage, theft, and vandalism. For the supply chain specifically, replacing a critical supplier identified as being at risk would be an example of a mitigation measure to eliminate a risk. Having a redundant (backup or alternate) source for the product or service provided by a potentially at-risk supplier is a measure to protect against impacts should the supplier go out of business. Based on a cost-benefit analysis, the selected mitigation steps must be cost-effective and must provide safeguards against one or more hazards.

The second component of the program, preparedness, includes all actions taken before a destructive or disruptive event occurs in order to lessen its impacts on the organization and its operations. This encompasses writing and testing plans, organizing and training teams to carry out those plans, and stocking and maintaining emergency supplies and equipment. For the supply chain, maintaining complete and current contact lists of all suppliers, contractors, transport companies, and others crucial to continued supply chain operations, as well as having off-site access to those lists, are valuable preparedness steps. Both mitigation and preparedness must be ongoing to meet an organization's changing needs, operations, financial situation, technology, competitive market, regulatory requirements, and industry conditions.

The actual response to a destructive or disruptive event—the third component of the program—often begins while the event is still occurring. This could include evacuating the building, accounting for employees and visitors, and obtaining necessary medical attention. For the supply chain, a response action could involve shutting down warehouse equipment before an evacuation. Also part of the response phase is the initial assessment of damage as well as actions taken to prevent further damage.

The final component of the program, recovery/continuity, may begin either before or immediately after the response phase is concluded, depending on the type of disaster, and would include any actions taken to work toward a normalization of operations in accordance with the priorities established and documented in the business continuity plan. This could include conducting an in-depth assessment of damage and operational impacts, notifying employees when to return to work, relocating operations and employees, or responding to media requests for information. A supply chain–specific continuity action could include establishing and maintaining contact with suppliers, customers, and carriers.

Each business unit is a unique operation and needs to be involved in the development and maintenance of the organization's business continuity program. A planning process that incorporates all levels of the company results in a continuity capability that both protects the organization and may serve as a competitive advantage.

To ensure the continued success of a business continuity program, it is essential that ongoing ownership and oversight of the program be specified in the plan and assigned to a position that reports directly to senior management. Such guidance and direction for a successful program is ensured through corporate-level planning standards and policies. Management's active commitment to the project and resulting business continuity program will provide support for the planning process and make available the required resources.

The Business Continuity Planning Process

While business continuity programs are ongoing, the initial planning process is a project with a specific objective, a defined start and end date, and, more often than not, limited resources.

Business continuity planning should be approached as you would any other project. A strong project manager ensures that the project stays on track regardless of its focus. Typically, a planning group—whether a team, task force, or committee—is involved, with its members working together to achieve a common goal, which is the development and implementation of a comprehensive continuity program. This team approach is valuable for several reasons. First and foremost, business continuity is enterprise-wide. Representation from all key departments provides a more inclusive perspective and an accurate understanding of the organization and its operations. The program then becomes one in which all business units have ownership. While this is not the primary rationale for having a planning team, this approach results in a sharing of the work involved. Once the team is established, using project management best practices helps steer the group through the continuity planning process.

Time invested at project initiation is well spent and pays dividends over the course of the project. This includes establishing the project process, scope, goals, and deliverables and identifying all participants: the executive sponsor, the individual responsible for review and approval, the planning group leader, group members, and go-to people for special requirements such as advice on legal issues. It also includes establishing the project schedule with a timeline, milestones, and a monitoring and reporting process.

Great assets that planning group members can bring to the project include the abilities to think critically, strategically, and creatively. The involvement of people throughout the organization with a certain level of understanding of continuity planning principles and process is necessary as well, to ensure that those assigned to the project have sufficient know-how to successfully complete the work required. This may necessitate some training, whether it's through reading books, taking formal classes, or attending workshops and seminars. Another approach is to have training presented in-house for the entire planning group.

Using a Consultant

In some cases, contracting with a consultant may be an advantageous solution to narrowing a knowledge and experience gap or to providing person-hours that employees do not have to dedicate to the project. The project plan should be reviewed in detail to determine when working with a consultant would be beneficial. This may be if outside assistance would be beneficial for the entire project, to facilitate the planning process, or only for certain project phases and tasks. You should also identify where in the scope of the project it is necessary to get a consultant's expertise, experience, guidance and direction, and unbiased perspective on the organization and its operations. It may be determined that a consultant is needed to facilitate the planning process, conduct the business impact analysis (BIA), or assist with the development of plan documents, or it may be determined that hands-on assistance is needed with each task of each project. If it is decided that hiring a consultant would be a good investment, the following tips can be helpful:

→ Make sure that the consultant won't recommend solutions or strategies that require purchasing products and services that the consultant provides or represents.

→ Avoid a situation where methodologies, documents, or other deliverables remain the property of the consultant rather than your organization.

→ Insist on a learn-as-you-go approach that results in a knowledge transfer at every step of the project. This helps your organization develop an internal capacity to maintain, update, and further enhance its business continuity capabilities without the need for the consultant to return year after year.

Using Software

Another consideration may be the use of a software package that automates many elements of the planning process, such as conducting a BIA. The number of new vendors and software packages skyrocketed after 9/11 and has continued to grow as business continuity is increasingly recognized as a fundamental element of good business management. Using one of these tools may be helpful in your planning process—with some caveats.

Software should not be allowed to drive the project. It is important to remember that software is a tool; it does not do the work. People do the work. Software does not gather the information needed for the BIA. In addition, various steps require a human component. These include following up with those who are less than timely in providing input, validating questionable responses to surveys, and getting more detailed information. Computers cannot develop insight as a result of life experience. People know their organization's operating environment, culture, and people—all key considerations when developing a business continuity program. Computers have no IQ, have no emotional intelligence competencies such as teamwork, collaboration, initiative, empathy, or motivation, and lack spontaneous interactivity capacity. Common sense, good judgment, and the mysterious process of intuition can be indispensable in finding and selecting the most appropriate continuity strategies.

While some software packages are more user-friendly than others, there is a learning curve for any new software. Providing training to the people who will be using it is critical, and this involves building training time into the project schedule. Without training, users will be slower in operating the software, make more errors, possibly become frustrated, and in a worst case doom the successful use of the software.

If, after analyzing the ins and outs of using a software package, the decision is to continue to investigate the possibilities, the real work begins as you prepare to select the best software for your organization. A selection committee should be established made up of representatives of all those who will be using the software, including the individual heading the project as well as team members and someone from your IT department with experience in evaluating software. An initial investigation of vendors and their software should be conducted by reviewing printed material and online information. Most software vendors are pleased to have an opportunity to provide a demo, which selection committee members can try out to get an initial impression of the product's capabilities and usability.

As a final check before a decision is made to purchase a software package, a cost-benefit analysis should be conducted to determine whether this is the best use of project dollars. This should include the following questions:

→ Does the software short-circuit the planning process, which can be equally as beneficial as the written plan?

→ Is there equal value from a computer-based BIA as with one conducted without the software?

→ Does the process still involve key people from all the business units?

→ Can you get a better return on the same amount of money by, for example, adding a full-time position or hiring a consultant?

After applying the criteria agreed upon at the beginning of the process, all vendors can be evaluated and your choice narrowed down to three to five. The finalists can then be invited to an interview where they have an opportunity to demonstrate the product, respond to questions and concerns, and discuss pricing. All costs, fees, and expense items—such as licensing fees, implementation assistance, initial and follow-up training, upgrades and enhancements, and support services—should be identified.

Work with the procurement department throughout the selection process to ensure that all company purchasing policies and procedures are being followed. Once a final selection has been made, procurement can assist with negotiating a contract that includes a detailed list of deliverables, warranties, and service level agreements and facilitate the contract approval process.

I am amazed when I listen to people from two organizations who are talking about software packages their companies purchased. One individual praises his company's package, while the other derides her company's package. Then I learn that they are talking about the same product. There are companies that have purchased such software but have not used it for anything except, perhaps, as a very expensive doorstop. There are any number of reasons for this, including a failure to select a package that is the best fit for the company, unrealistic expectations about what the software can do, or a belief that the software will replace the need for people to be involved in the project.

A well-chosen software package can be an excellent tool to assist in conducting the BIA or other project tasks. But whether or not you opt to use software, it is the people involved in the project—their intelligence, knowledge of the organization, creativity, and blood, sweat, and tears—that ultimately determine the success of your BIA and the resulting business continuity program.

Beginning the Project

In preparation to begin the project:

→ Determine exactly what is currently in place and what must be developed.

→ Gather necessary documents such as any existing business continuity or related plans like emergency response plans, security plans, and company policies that relate to the upcoming project.

→ Identify all regulatory, legal, and industry business continuity requirements.

→ Confer with the person who manages the company's insurance program to gain an understanding of current coverage.

Despite the application of best business continuity and project management practices, continuity planning can still fail. To help ensure a successful end product and an optimum outcome, lay the groundwork at the beginning of the project:

→ Establish the project's scope and a realistic and attainable project schedule. This avoids misunderstandings about what will and will not be accomplished and avoids having to take dangerous shortcuts in order to meet an unrealistic timeline.

→ Ensure that sufficient resources are dedicated to the project, including project team members with the necessary skills and knowledge and a budget that covers all reasonable expenses associated with the planning process. This avoids having to ask for additional resources, which can delay or derail the project.

→ Kick off the project with an announcement made by the project's executive sponsor or senior-level executive. Evidence of top management's support validates the project and encourages participation.

→ From the start, communicate the business continuity project throughout the organization to ensure that all managers and other employees understand the project, its purpose, its impacts, and what is expected of them. Doing so encourages cooperation and prevents rumors and misinformation.

At the launch of a business continuity project, there are two known factors that are the initial focal point of the planning process: (1) the organization as it exists and (2) the risks that currently pose a potential threat to the organization and its operations. From there, an effective comprehensive continuity planning process enters the assessment phase, which includes understanding current capabilities, conducting a hazard assessment, and conducting a BIA. These best practice activities are the foundation of the continuity planning process.

Figure 3-1 represents the business continuity planning lifecycle, an ongoing process of continuity planning that includes the development, maintenance, and testing of business continuity plans to ensure a continually maintained and enhanced business continuity capability. The ongoing lifecycle starts with a hazard assessment and mitigation and then continues through the BIA, development of business continuity strategies, development of business continuity plans and procedures, and the testing and implementation of the plans.

Note that the steps in the planning lifecycle are not numbered. Business continuity planning is not a first step to last step, check-the-box undertaking. Once the initial program is developed, there must be an ongoing process to continually maintain and increase disaster management capability through ongoing review and revision in order to further develop a sustainable, mature program. Without assigned responsibility for maintaining the program and fostering continuity awareness throughout the organization, even blue ribbon programs ultimately fail.

The hazard assessment and BIA are the analysis stage

FIGURE 3-1.

BUSINESS CONTINUITY PLANNING LIFECYCLE.

An Ongoing Process

of the project. They serve as the basis for developing the strategies that will be documented in business continuity plans and detailed procedures.

Hazard Assessment

The purpose of the hazard assessment is to gain an understanding of the disasters for which the organization must plan and to establish what level of risk the organization can accept. Conducting this assessment involves three steps:

1. *Identifying the organization's threats and vulnerabilities.* What can go wrong?
2. *Analyzing the identified vulnerabilities.* What is the likelihood it will go wrong?
3. *Assessing the resulting impact.* What are the consequences if it goes wrong?

This process requires making some assumptions and doing some forecasting. As a result, it is a certainty that your assumptions will be less than 100 percent accurate, and they may be off by as much as 10 to 20 percent or more. While not perfect, the hazard assessment does produce an increased understanding of the threats to the company and the impact of those threats to critical operations. Based on the results of the hazard assessment, identified risks are mitigated to the extent both possible and practical. Conducting a hazard assessment can be complex, time-consuming, and expensive. However, it is an essential component of the planning process. Figure 3-2 can be a useful tool for identifying the hazards for which mitigation and planning are most needed.

The first step is listing all known hazards and risks. Then, each of the risks should be graphed by two factors:

1. On a scale of 0 (low) to 10 (high), how probable is it that the disaster will occur? (This probability is graphed along the y axis.)
2. On a scale of 0 (none) to 10 (severe), should it occur, what will be the impact of the disaster on the organization and its operations? (This impact is graphed along the x axis.)

Hazards in the upper right quadrant are those that are both most likely to occur and result in the most severe damage, making them the greatest risks to the organization. These hazards are the initial focus of mitigation and planning.

Conversely, the hazards in the lower left quadrant are

FIGURE 3-2.

HAZARD ASSESSMENT GRAPH.

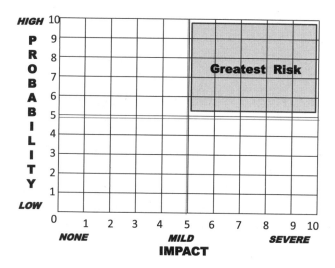

the least likely to occur and are not likely to result in significant damage or operation disruption. Managing these low-risk hazards can be delayed and in the interim may be resolved by the planning and mitigation done for the hazards that pose the greatest risk.

Business Impact Analysis

The business impact analysis is a process used to identify mission-critical business functions, which may also be referred to as time-critical business functions. The BIA identifies the internal and external dependencies of each of the identified functions, establishes a priority order in which to restore them, identifies resources needed for each of these functions (such as facilities, personnel, equipment, electronic data, paper records, and software), and develops a target time frame for the full restoration of each. The results of the BIA are used as a basis for developing business continuity strategies.

Some of the BIA deliverables have value-added benefits above and beyond their use in continuity planning. Documented processes, detailed descriptions of individual business functions, identification of interdependencies, and process flow charts that are developed in the BIA process are all useful well beyond the business continuity planning process.

Strategy Development

Business continuity strategies are developed to support the results of the impact analysis. Because formulating continuity strategies tackles need-to-survive rather than business-as-normal challenges, a different mindset is necessary. Developing strategies needed to resume or maintain all identified critical business functions and processes can be daunting. An uncomplicated way to begin is by starting with the functions identified in the BIA results as most critical, and then for each, identifying how to ensure backups or substitutes for:

→ *People Who Carry Out the Identified Critical Functions.* Who can step in if the people who have primary responsibility for these functions are not available?

→ *Facilities Where the Critical Functions Take Place.* Where can they be relocated if the primary facility is lost or inaccessible?

→ *Critical Business Processes.* Is there a temporary substitute if the primary process is unavailable, or can one be quickly established?

Plan Development

Successful business continuity efforts result from an analysis of possible situations and the development and proper testing and execution of plans and procedures. Business continuity plans are written to document the program and its strategies and then serve as its operations manual.

As a result of an ever changing environment, constantly

evolving technology, unforeseen circumstances and events, and other variables, plans will not always be 100 percent spot-on as developed. They are, however, the key to a greatly increased probability for the more rapid and successful continuity of business operations following a disaster.

A business continuity plan formalizes and codifies continuity policies and standards. At a minimum, the plan documents:

→ What needs to be done
→ How it will be done
→ Where it will be done
→ When it will be done
→ Who will do it

While there are standards and best practices in developing plan documents, each plan must be developed specifically for the organization. One size does not fit all. Taking another organization's plan or a plan template and simply changing names, contact information, and locations is a recipe for failure; it will not work and will likely create additional problems beyond the initial disaster.

If the organization is of substantial size or complexity, has multiple locations, or is a global or multinational company, more than one plan may be needed. Fully meeting the company's business continuity needs requires a coordinated "family of plans" starting at the top level of the organization:

→ *Corporate business continuity plan.* The umbrella plan for the organization, the corporate plan documents the organization's continuity program purpose, scope, policies, standards, and expectations, as well as the business continuity organization and reporting structure. Requirements for testing, training, plan reviews, and updates are detailed. The plan establishes procedures for how the board or upper level management will assess the long-term impacts of the disaster event on operations and provide advice and counsel for those carrying out business continuity plans throughout the organization. This plan may include guidelines for communicating with the press, the media, and—in global organizations—government agencies in countries where company facilities are located. Plans at all other levels throughout the organization follow the requirements and protocols set forth in the corporate plan.

→ *Division, site, or geographical business continuity plans.* These plans are often location-specific and, therefore, include procedures for responding to the hazards and potential disasters that may impact the site. Critical functions performed may also differ, and specific procedures and strategies needed to continue or resume operations at the location are outlined. Site plans follow all guidelines set forth in the corporate business continuity plan and coordinate the department plans within the division.

→ *Department business continuity plans.* Department plans contain clear, detailed strategies and procedures needed to continue or resume operations or provide services in the event of a disaster that compromises the ability of the department to carry out its identified critical functions within the recovery time objective. Supply chain department plans include procedures to be followed to fully restore supply chain operations in the event of an interruption. The IT department's disaster recovery plan is its business continuity plan.

→ *Field operations business continuity plans, if applicable.* Field operations plans provide guidance for employees such as service providers or field technicians working away from the organization's facilities. These plans outline procedures that workers are to follow when a disaster occurs either in the field or at a company facility and that establish communications procedures to ensure that employees are kept informed of response and recovery efforts.

This multilevel integrated approach allows for the activation of business continuity plans appropriate to the severity of the disaster and resulting impact on operations. Based on assessment at the time of an event, full or partial activation is initiated. For example, the destruction of the only facility where core business functions such as data processing and finance are conducted would likely require full activation at all levels. On the other hand, a small fire in a warehouse causing minor damage and resulting in no injuries, limited impact on operations, and no media attention might only require activation of the site plan.

Smaller organizations or organizations with a single location or very few facilities that are all located within a small geographical area may need only one plan, perhaps with a plan annex covering detailed procedures for individual departments or work units.

A well-crafted plan should be complete enough and easy enough to use that those not involved in its development can run with it to get the organization back in business.

Program Testing and Implementation

Once strategies have been developed and plans have been written, all elements of the program are implemented. This includes publishing and distributing the initial plan document and providing the appropriate level of training for all employees to enable them to carry out their business continuity role, however great or small.

Testing is conducted to validate that strategies meet the organization's expectations and the plans accurately reflect strategies and provide sufficient guidance for those who will carry out the plans when a disaster occurs. It is only through testing that it is possible to identify insufficiencies or inaccuracies in plans and procedures and to determine whether carrying out the plans will allow operational recovery within the recovery time objectives. A first test of a new plan is almost certain to uncover needed revisions and enhancements.

Continuing to build program awareness and ongoing efforts to incorporate the program into the organization's culture and day-to-day business operations are also important considerations when rolling out a new program.

Undertaking the tasks required to complete the initial continuity planning lifecycle can be daunting even for those experienced in such planning. It can be more so for those charged with developing and maintaining a business continuity program while maintaining a full schedule of day-to-day duties in today's do-more-with-less business environment. Too often, the sheer volume of information that must be collected and processed seems overwhelming, and continuity planning must compete with other priorities. This can lead to false assumptions, rushed strategizing, and an untested and unworkable plan, or even worse: a planning project that gets put on the back burner, perhaps indefinitely.

There is a quote from the philosopher Voltaire that seems appropriate when considering the challenges of instituting a business continuity program. Roughly translated from the French, it reminds us that "The perfect is the enemy of the good." The inability to get a perfect program in place in a short time should not be allowed to stop the planning process. Even a partial program results in an increased capability to manage disasters. Each step taken to prepare the organization to manage its risks is a step in the right direction in developing business continuity competency.

Avoiding Business Continuity Silos

All organizations are symbiotic. Each business unit supports all others either directly or indirectly; no one unit is able to do the organization's work alone. Every organization is a complex interrelated grouping of business functions and activities. To remove any single unit unquestionably over a period of time causes operational slowdowns and bottlenecks, deterioration in the quality of the product or service, a financial hardship, and ultimately a total loss of the ability of the organization as a whole to function or deliver its product or service. To establish and maintain viable business continuity capability, all areas of the organization must be included.

The supply chain is a critical part of the organization's operations and, conversely, all other business functions within the organization—even those not directly tied to supply chain business units—are critical for continued supply chain operations. While payroll may be the first identified non–supply chain business function to come to mind, marketing, facilities, human resources, and research and development are some of the other business units that are essential to continued supply chain operations.

Supply chain professionals realize that this necessarily cooperative, mutually beneficial, and interdependent working relationship is even broader than internal operations. Perhaps more than others within an organization, those involved in supply chain operations realize that businesses do not operate in isolation and that not all critical functions are internal. They see on a daily basis that each and every part of the external supply chain network is potentially as critical to continued operations as is each of the internal business units.

A Holistic Approach to Risk Management

Business continuity as part of an all-inclusive approach to managing risk needs to be viewed not as a separate process or activity but as a competency that is embedded in the organization, its operations, and its culture. Better decisions are made when planning is built into existing business functions so that it becomes an inherent part of key decision-making processes.

Responsibility for managing an organization's risks may be scattered among several departments and functions. As previously stated, in organizations that first developed disaster recovery plans and later added a continuity program, it is not uncommon for IT to be assigned the added responsibility of developing and maintaining business continuity. Other departments may have responsibility for some part of the company's continuing efforts to manage all types of disasters. If this is done with a less than perfectly coordinated integrated effort, it can result in possible gaps or overlaps.

A slowly building trend in recent years, particularly in larger corporations, is to combine business continuity, disaster recovery, security, risk management/insurance, safety, etc., into one department with the head of the department reporting to an upper-level executive—for example, the CEO or COO. While it may at first seem that there is no direct relationship between these areas of an organization, on reflection, it should be clear that each function has a role to play in the continued well-being of the organization and its employees. Perhaps in the future it will not be unusual to see a new executive function and title— chief risk manager or chief risk officer (**CRO**)—for the person who is charged with managing all types of risks enterprise-wide. (See Figure 3-3.)

FIGURE 3-3.

A HOLISTIC INTEGRATED APPROACH TO MANAGING RISKS.

Wherever the business continuity function fits within the organization, it is critical that the program is given the full support and commitment of those at the executive level. In addition, the person heading it should have full accessibility to key decision makers.

Going Forward

It is not uncommon to find that a business continuity planning process was conducted without input from supply chain business units and that the resulting plans do not include supply chain continuity strategies. To improve supply chain continuity it is important to know to what extent the supply chain was included in the planning process.

→ Meet with the person responsible for your organization's business continuity program to learn more about the planning process currently being used.

→ Determine which supply chain business units were considered in the planning process and to what degree.

→ Learn how supply chain–related information was gathered and from whom.

→ If a supply chain representative is not currently a member of the planning group, suggest that one be assigned to actively participate in the planning process and serve as a liaison to coordinate the planning process in supply chain–related departments.

CHAPTER 4

The Organization, the Supply Chain, and Business Continuity

UPPLY CHAINS HAVE EVOLVED into far-reaching, complex, multitiered, demand-driven supply networks. As a result, the ways in which supply chain risks were managed in the past, if managed at all, do not work today. A new standard for supply chain risk management is required. Suppliers have their own tiers of subsuppliers, increased outsourcing of supply chain processes, and contracting out of manufacturing operations. They therefore must be viewed in terms of the accompanying greater risks and less direct control. Even a disaster in a seemingly less critical, remote part of the chain can result in a supply chain interruption that can lead to a failure to meet customer expectations. Distribution sector businesses such as distributors, retailers, and food and beverage companies are uniquely vulnerable to the effects of disruptions as service interruptions result in a rapid and extreme impact on end customer satisfaction, which can lead to long-term bottom line implications.

While there have been encouraging changes, such as the trend toward development of more constructive supplier relationships and increased supply chain transparency, there has also been a significant lag in attention to supply chain business continuity. Until as recently as the past five years or so, even some of the most business continuity–savvy organizations have turned their heads and crossed their fingers in the hope that supply chain disasters would steer clear of their companies until they "get around to" extending continuity programs to fully incorporate the supply chain. It is a risky proposition to adopt the approach of an ostrich with its head in the sand. No company can afford continued delays in implementing an enterprise-wide proactive approach to managing supply chain risks.

Enterprise-Wide Disaster Readiness

Business continuity planning is a core business practice. Being fully prepared to respond to disasters requires creating a program with an enterprise-wide focus that considers each aspect of the organization. As businesses are symbiotic, with each business unit supporting all others, all areas of the organization must be included to meet a goal of keeping the operation going. This integrated approach to business continuity requires that business units merge any stand-alone efforts into a cohesive and proactive plan.

Unilateral planning, while not totally ineffective, can lead to planning gaps, overlaps, false assumptions, and conflicts. As an example, let's say it is common knowledge among all departments located at a company's headquarters that, in a nearby town, the company has another facility that is not fully occupied and has seventy-five fully equipped and unused workspaces. In their individual plans, ten departments detail procedures for relocating key employees in the event that a disaster renders the headquarters uninhabitable. Each department plans to move twenty-five employees into the second facility, where they will resume what have been identified as critical business functions. Simply doing the math tells us this won't work. Without integrated, coordinated planning, it is possible that with the full activation of business continuity plans, 250 employees would show up at the second facility, each expecting to use one of the seventy-five available workspaces.

To be truly effective, not only must every business unit be considered, but there must be planning integration among all components of the external support services—such as financial institutions, supply chain partners, and electric, water, and telecommunications service providers—as well as among the interdependent functions within the company's own facilities.

Incorporating the Supply Chain in Business Continuity Planning: An Integrated Approach

Every business is a web of interdependencies, and the larger the organization, the more complex the web. A seemingly minor glitch in one business unit can have a rapid domino effect on every other part of the business. Yet it is still not unusual to find that an organization has a business continuity program that excludes one or more elements of the business. These left-behind functions often include supply chain components or the entire supply chain operation. In these organizations, supply chain departments are involved only when a disaster that impacts the supply chain occurs. This results in an ad hoc, seat-of-the-pants response to disasters that is more time-consuming, less effective, and usually much more costly.

Done well, business continuity planning and management is a tremendously powerful and effective process that often goes well beyond its core goals. In addition to developing a capability to manage operational risks, improvements in processes can be identified. For the supply chain, this can mean finding ways to streamline the supply chain itself, strengthen customer-supplier relationships, and discover potential cost savings. Stakeholder expectations must be met even if transportation routes into and out of the business's primary location are closed for two days, two weeks, two months, or even longer. The business must be prepared to survive even when critical inventory cannot be replenished through normal channels for such a period of time.

Today's supply chain professionals need to have—at a minimum—an understanding of business continuity basics and the organization's business continuity approach and strategies. Regardless of the level of active involvement in the planning process or the assigned role in carrying out the plans, knowing where their business unit fits in the big picture of the organization's continuity strategies is essential knowledge for every supply chain manager.

First-rate supply chain management (SCM) and business continuity are inseparably connected. To evaluate the accuracy of this statement, we will use the following description of SCM: the process of planning and processing orders received; handling, transporting, and storing all materials, components, and products purchased, processed, or distributed; and managing inventories in a systematic, coordinated manner among all the components of the chain to fulfill customers' orders upon receipt. Based on this definition, a primary goal of supply chain management is to ensure that the supply chain and all the business functions and activities in the supply chain, internal and external, are *working at an acceptable level to respond to customer orders*. It then follows that supply chain business continuity is essential to supply chain management's ability to fully meet its responsibilities.

Even within the supply chain itself, there are cases where supply chain continuity does not fully incorporate all the functions within the supply chain, either internally or externally. While expanding the business continuity view outward to suppliers and others is a must, it is equally important that the supply chain avoid a silo approach to business continuity planning and take into account all internal supply chain interdependencies. Warehouses and distribution centers, manufacturing, and procurement and purchasing are a few examples of the internal functions that must be involved.

Warehouses and Distribution Centers

Warehouses are an integral part of the supply chain, whether they are a single building or many buildings at multiple locations, whether owned or outsourced. Warehouses were once viewed only as storage buildings that housed incoming materials and parts and finished products waiting to be shipped. Today, however, they are highly sophisticated systems that not only receive and track incoming raw materials and components and store and stage outbound merchandise for delivery but also use highly sophisticated technical systems to process orders, track deliveries, and maintain accurate, up-to-date inventory records. This strategic and critically important element of the supply chain must be included in the business continuity planning process. An inability of the warehouse to function at an acceptable level can lead to a failure to meet delivery requirements and create a production stoppage.

Manufacturing

Manufacturing is perhaps the most difficult of the supply chain elements for which to develop continuity strategies. This difficulty can result in an incorrect and risky decision to exclude manufacturing units from the planning process. This may seem ironic in the case of companies for which the production or assembly of an end product is the source of income. It is likely that the complexity and limited continuity strategy options for many manufacturing operations, coupled with the fact that few major manufacturers in the United States have suffered recent catastrophic losses, make it tempting to avoid the issue altogether. Just some of the specific planning challenges in the development of manufacturing continuity include the following:

→ The possible need to replace customized manufacturing components and custom fixtures that can take a considerable amount of time

→ The expense of equipment and tools, which can be prohibitive in stockpiling a backup supply

→ Lack of available alternate sites for relocating manufacturing operations that require clean air quality or an antistatic environment in the event the primary facility is destroyed, damaged, or uninhabitable

→ Chemicals used in some processes that are hazardous materials, creating additional risks and challenges should it be necessary to relocate a manufacturing process

→ Federal, state, and local regulatory and licensing requirements that may require inspections and reevaluation, leading to additional delays in restoring operations

→ The fact that testing manufacturing continuity plans and strategies is often limited in order to avoid having to shut down and restart production lines

Developing business continuity strategies for manufacturing operations is challenging, yet it must not be omitted. It requires creative out-of-the-box problem solving and strategy development to ensure that the bread and butter of a manufacturing operation can continue or be quickly restored following a disaster event.

Procurement and Purchasing

The responsibilities of procurement and purchasing are critical considerations in the continuity planning process, whether these functions are one or two business units in an organization. People with procurement responsibilities are central in the ongoing selection of suppliers that meet business continuity–related requirements. Purchasing plays a key role in obtaining supplies, equipment, and services identified in the planning process. It plays an even more critical role following a disaster, when it is necessary to quickly obtain supplies and equipment to support getting the business back up and running. Depending on the type of disaster and its severity, what may be needed may include:

→ Disaster debris removal and disposal services

→ Heavy equipment rental

→ Services such as cleaning, water removal, mold remediation, and building repair

→ Generator and other equipment rentals

→ Office furniture and equipment rental or purchase

→ Office supplies

→ Mobile phones or phone cards

→ A moving company

→ Structural engineers

Part of the continuity planning process may be to develop more flexible and streamlined purchasing policies and processes that can be implemented following a disaster in order to more quickly obtain goods and services necessary to maintain or restore critical operations as quickly as practicable.

The Value of Unilateral Continuity Planning

It is necessary to look beyond the supply chain for a continuity program to fully succeed in meeting the goal of ensuring that the organization can avoid lengthy operational disruptions. As mentioned at the start of this chapter, each business unit must be part of an enterprise-wide continuity program that takes a big picture, process-based approach.

Even if there is no company-wide business continuity program, there is still value in developing a stand-alone supply chain business continuity plan. However, missing from this single business unit approach are corporate-level functions such as media relations and the ability to quickly go through channels to get approvals for additional financial support. While far from ideal, department plans enable the supply chain to continue or more quickly recover than if there are no plans at all, particularly when the disaster impacts only a localized, supply chain functional unit. Although it takes longer to get back up to speed and requires more effort, supply chain–only plans do provide guidance and direction to those working to get the supply chain moving again following a disaster. In addition, once department-centric plans are developed, they often serve as a model and become the impetus for the rest of the organization to begin the planning process.

Continuity of the supply chain is more complex and challenging today than ever before. Many things contribute to an environment where a disruption of the supply chain that was once considered an inconvenience is now viewed as unacceptable. These factors include just-in-time inventories and longer, leaner, and more complex supply chains that may rely on out-of-area and out-of-country suppliers, stringent service level agreements, an increasingly greater number of new products, extended hours of operations, and greater regulatory requirements. And in today's challenging economic times, even greater pressure is being exerted on supply chains as a result of efforts to minimize costs and cope with an unstable economy that results in pricing and credit concerns and adds concerns about the continued existence of critical suppliers and service providers. And lest we forget, our supply chains need not only be lean but also be green, sustainable, and resilient.

Assessing Current Preparedness

A key initial step in the process to develop a new program to manage supply chain risks or expand or improve an existing one is to completely and honestly assess the organization's current business continuity capabilities. Often there are misconceptions about the actual level of business continuity preparedness within the organization. Upon investigation, the reality may be that while a plan does exist, it documents only the strategies for recovering the company's technology—in other words, a disaster recovery plan. Even if the plan seems to involve the entire enterprise, it may have been created only to meet a requirement from a customer or auditors and have been written in a vacuum with no planning process and no program. It also may be the case that there is a plan document that was completed well over a year ago, has never been tested, and has not been reviewed or updated since it was completed. In reality, this is not a viable plan, let alone a program. It is only printed pages in a binder.

You may hear a manager state confidently, "We will get everything back up and running within a day, maybe even less." The actuality may be that it will take at least forty-eight to seventy-two hours to fully activate the entire plan or to recover the most critical data center functions. Or you may be told, "We know that our business continuity plan is a good one. We were recently audited and our plan passed with flying colors." If you hear this, check to determine what type of audit was conducted. It may have been only a checklist audit, verifying only that a plan document exists. It's important to know if the audit considered whether the plan has been tested and if so, when it was tested. Equally important is whether the auditor determined to what extent people were trained to carry out the plan.

The potential success of a program can be evaluated and measured by conducting an ongoing series of regularly scheduled tests and exercises that determine whether the plan's stated objectives can be met. The capability to continue or resume operations, staff critical functions, meet recovery time objectives for IT support services, and maintain an appropriate level of communication with all stakeholders are just some of the areas that may be evaluated in the testing process.

Some organizations opt to apply a more sophisticated system of metrics and reporting as a way to further measure business continuity program competency and maturity. Data is gathered to measure business continuity factors such as the number of months between plan reviews and updates, the frequency of employee training, the number of tests and exercises scheduled and carried out each year, the number of business units participating in tests, and the level of success in achieving the recovery time objectives during a test. Factors can be assigned a relative weight, and benchmarks are established against which scores are compared. A metrics scorecard provides a standardized measurement of program success that is particularly useful in large organizations with multitiered business continuity organizations.

Whether a testing program, metrics, or a combination of both is used to measure business continuity capability, to be effective there needs to be a requirement for executive review and sign-off on the resulting reports. A reasonable expectation would then seem to be that the reviewing executive require that any necessary revisions, improvements, and enhancements be made.

To help you gauge your organization's current level of business continuity preparedness, refer to Appendix A, which contains a business continuity planning assessment. While this assessment is not all-inclusive, it does provide an approximate evaluation of existing capability.

Going Forward

Business continuity relates specifically to the continuation and survival of the core functions of the *entire enterprise*. An isolated silo approach to business continuity management can result in an incomplete continuity program that can fall short of establishing comprehensive and integrated strategies and plans that support business survivability following a disaster.

Just as it is necessary to have all the pieces of a puzzle in order to put it together, having all business units included in continuity planning is essential to fully restoring the business when disaster strikes.

→ Complete the Business Continuity Planning Assessment for your organization (Appendix A).

→ Ask colleagues to complete the assessment as well. Then discuss the results.

→ Outline how the business continuity needs of the supply chain are in synch with and support the company's strategic goals.

→ Review existing business continuity policies and plans to make sure your business unit and all supply chain business units were addressed in the planning process and are included in plan documents.

CHAPTER 5

Risk Identification and Hazard Assessment

I N ORDER TO EFFECTIVELY manage supply chain risk, you must first know what the risks are and fully understand their impact. A *hazard assessment* (or *risk analysis* or *assessment*) is conducted to identify the potential threats to the organization, quantify the impact of those risks on core business functions, document the threats, and then develop an approach for eliminating or decreasing the impact of the recognized threats. A hazard assessment and a business impact analysis are the two keystones of the business continuity planning lifecycle. (Business impact analysis is the subject of Chapter 6.)

A frequently cited quote from writer Frederick B. Wilcox reminds us that "You can't steal second base and keep your foot on first," and it is a generally accepted reality that risk is inherent in all aspects of business operations and that an *acceptable level of risk* is necessary for progress and achievement. The purpose of a hazard assessment and accompanying mitigation program is not to eliminate all hazards. A business certainly cannot function within the confines of a protective bubble, and even if it were possible to eliminate all current risks, new threats would continue to surface. The goal of business continuity is to identify all known threats, determine the organization's acceptable level of risk or operational threshold of pain, and, based on that information, manage risks to a level that moves the organization closer to a goal of developing a capability to continue or quickly restore critical business functions when disasters occur.

There are three key ways in which the results of the hazard assessment are used:

1. To identify the vulnerabilities requiring the most immediate and extensive business continuity planning and act as guide for prioritizing the order in which risks are addressed
2. To provide a basis for developing a mitigation program to eliminate potential disasters as possible and lessen the impact of those that cannot be eliminated
3. To provide a foundation for the business continuity planning process

Once we have identified and quantified the threats that are most likely to occur and those that would create the greatest disruption to the company's operations, it is then possible to determine how to most effectively manage them. Among the choices are absorbing the risk, transferring the risk, or reducing the impact of the risk through mitigation.

As the past does not necessarily predict the future and there is no way to see what the future has in store, conducting a hazard assessment does require some subjectivity and can never be totally accurate. Yet it goes far beyond the simple, reasonable assumption that your organization will experience a disaster at some point in the future. If implemented correctly, a hazard assessment provides invaluable planning guidance through a logical process of identifying, rationally evaluating, and addressing risks and their impacts, and it thereby avoids planning based on a lack of information, assumptions, or misinformation.

The Changing Face of Supply Chain Risks

Supply chains have never been so sophisticated or complex and, as a result, so vulnerable to risk. The lean production method introduced by production improvement expert and quality control pioneer W. Edwards Deming, as well as just-in-time inventories, less vertical integration, dependence on single-source suppliers, and mounting reliance on cost-reducing suppliers often located in unstable areas of the globe, all contribute to a higher level of risk.

Many supply chain threats are not local to an organization. Globalization has led to lower production costs resulting from cheap labor and materials, along with added risks resulting from extended supply chains, decreased reliability, language barriers, suppliers' further outsourcing the work, and transparency issues. Add to this mix terrorist threats, political unrest, shutdowns at shipping facilities, and economic instability. The end result is a recipe for potentially significant and long-term supply chain interruptions that have the potential to cascade across the organization and result in the loss of business and customers, severe long-term damage to reputation, and legal action.

Today, countless manufacturing companies actually produce very little. Rather, they purchase components and parts from multiple suppliers for assembly and distribution, creating a tremendous dependency on their supply networks. The ongoing push for a smaller physical footprint is often accomplished by streamlining the company's facilities by removing operations and locations seen as being redundant, inefficient, or unnecessary. This results in having more eggs in fewer baskets.

The Effects of Natural Disasters

Of course, organizations whose operations are solely within national borders are also not immune to a changing disaster landscape. In the United States, for instance, the first decade of the millennium brought natural disasters that, while not necessarily unpredictable, were unprecedented in their magnitude and scope. While the Gulf States are all too familiar with hurricanes and flooding in the Midwest (particularly along the Mississippi) is a fact of life, two destructive events are examples of natural disasters that resulted in severe supply chain disruptions.

In 2005, Hurricane Katrina—one of the largest natural disasters in the history of the United States—destroyed key shipping and hauling infrastructure along the Gulf Coast from Florida to Texas. Rail and truck routes were closed, bridges were severely damaged or destroyed, and barge traffic was delayed. These transportation disruptions caused a frantic rush to recover and restore deliveries. Ports such as New Orleans, one of the world's largest, were also impacted, leaving thousands of tons of goods and materials damaged or destroyed. This included forestry-related products, aluminum, natural rubber, and coffee.

The other destructive event was record severe flooding along the Mississippi in 2008, which destroyed rail bridges and washed out track, closed truck routes creating detours as long as 150 miles or more, and brought barge traffic to a near standstill. At one point, it was estimated that hundreds of railcars were backed up and as many as 100 barges were idled on a 300-mile stretch of the Mississippi. Some carriers placed embargos on deliveries. The immediate and ripple effects on companies along the Mississippi that are dependent on river traffic to move goods were enormous and included increased shipping costs as a result of the necessity to rely more on truck transit and less on intermodal delivery and in some cases varying lengths of closures of factories and other businesses.

Hazard Assessments and Understanding Threats from Disasters

A hazard assessment makes possible a more complete understanding of the threats that can impact the organization's ability to function as intended and provides a framework within which to continue the planning process.

We know that "things" happen. In some cases, what makes an emergency a disaster is not knowing exactly what its severity or scope will be or when it will happen. In other cases, disasters not only are not on our radar screens; we could not even have imagined them in our worst nightmares. We must understand that in today's uncertain times, there will always be new disasters we have not previously considered as the spectrum of threats to supply chain operations continues to change and expand, and both new risks that were previously not considered and long-known disasters create more damage and disruption than ever before. As a result, once the initial business continuity program is in place, it is important to regularly revisit the planning process to update the hazard assessment to reflect new threats and changes in the level of impact each threat will have on operations.

Identifying Supply Chain Risks

From a supply chain perspective, any event is a threat with the full potential to become a disaster if it results in a significant disruption of transportation, loss of inventory, the inability of suppliers to fulfill orders, the inability of the organization to fulfill orders, or the inability to communicate with customers, suppliers, transportation providers, or other stakeholders.

Internal and External Risks

In the past, it was a common practice for the hazard assessment process to focus almost exclusively on the most direct threats facing a company, such as a large and damaging fire in a building, a hurricane or earthquake, or a serious failure in the data center. But today, threats to the overall organization are also risks for the internal supply chain business units. Moreover, the supply chain has its own set of very inherent risks, many of which exist outside the organization. While some disasters may directly impact only the supply chain and may even be external to the organization, they must be fully considered for a hazard assessment to completely succeed in its purpose. The larger the enterprise, the greater the number of companies included in its supply chain and the greater the number of tiers all contributing to the number of potential risks. (The tiers include tier one suppliers that provide finished components, tier two suppliers that provide subcomponents or parts directly to tier one suppliers, tier three suppliers that provide raw materials to tier two suppliers, and so forth.) The more tiers, the greater the possibility that an event impacting a subsupplier may have a domino effect that accumulates into a major disruption for the customer company, or that a combination of small events may occur along the supply chain that culminate in a disaster before reaching the last link in the chain. Though indirect threats, such as the loss of a key supplier or a transportation interruption, can have an equal or more damaging impact on the continuity of the supply chain, these risks are often ignored or overlooked in the hazard assessment process.

Large-scale supply chain disruptions may be infrequent. Yet today, the risks increase, and the effects of a seeming minor disruption can be devastating. Risks lurk along the entire length and breadth of our often nontransparent supply chains. As a result of diverse sourcing locations for some companies, in particular those operating globally, shipping delays may be common, with causes as varied as natural disasters, political instability, labor union actions, exchange rate fluctuations, or capacity issues. Other threats include security issues in less stable countries, weather, shipping congestion, and equipment failures. Risk levels are increased when there is total reliance on a sole source provider or shipper.

Hazard Identification Process

The first step in the hazard assessment is to identify all risks, whether natural (such as hurricanes, earthquakes, and severe winter storms), technological (such as engineering failures, equipment failures, and power outages), or of human causes (such as arson, acts of terrorism, cyber attacks, and riots). None of us has perfect foresight, and while the past is not always the best way of knowing what will happen in the future, it can help us identify potential disasters. Companies in areas where there has been widespread flooding need to consider if future flooding may reach their location. The proximity to an earthquake fault line is a definite consideration. Organizations located in areas that have experienced wild land fires need to consider this hazard even though they may not have had facilities destroyed or damaged by past occurrences. All these and other hazards must be identified, both for internal operations and for outside entities upon which there is a dependency.

While hazards should be considered in a broad context, you should try to identify events that may actually occur. While anything is possible, the likelihood of a tsunami in Kansas does not merit consideration. If your organization has facilities in different geographic locations, a hazard assessment must be conducted to identify the varying hazards for each.

Do not overlook the obvious. I recall sitting in a conference with a client's planning team at the beginning stage of conducting a hazard assessment. Everyone was contributing to the list of the company's possible disasters. Throughout the process, I kept expecting someone to mention a threat that seemed evident to me as I heard the frequent and unmistakable sound of airplanes overhead. The business was located within the takeoff and landing patterns of three major metropolitan airports. Yet because the employees heard the noise of the planes on a daily basis, no one thought much about it, let alone considered the planes as a potential threat.

The same holds true for not-so-obvious nearby hazards. A gas refinery, a major highway or railway used to transport hazardous materials, or a business or government agency that may be the target for sabotage or terrorism can create a risk for your company simply due to proximity.

In short, all supply chain risks should be included in your assessment. For all entities in the chain—including suppliers, contractors, vendors, and transporters—be aware of their financial and stability issues and of the stability of your suppliers' raw material supplies. The more critical the business partner, the greater the need to assess and manage the associated hazards.

Prodromes—events that might be indicators that warn that a disaster may occur either in the future or under slightly different circumstances—need to be identified as well. For example, let's say shipments from a critical supplier whose deliveries have previously always been on time suddenly begin to be sporadically late. This happens more frequently, and the lag times become increasingly longer. These late deliveries are prodromes and might be early warning signs of a potential threat that needs to be managed before the situation becomes a disaster. All supplier-related risks should be identified and included in the hazard assessment.

It is also important to collect information from multiple sources. There are many different types of threats that must be considered, and no single source of information can include them all. Different sources identify different sets of risks to add to the assessment. Public safety officials and emergency agencies can provide valuable input and data, as can internal experts such as security, safety, facilities, and human resources.

After identifying all the possible threats to your business, consider how likely it is that the threat will occur. Finally, and perhaps most important, consider: Should this event occur, what will the impact likely be on your ability to continue your day-to-day business operations.

Conducting a hazard assessment requires making some assumptions, such as the likelihood that an identified threat will actually occur, and doing some forecasting. It is important to remember that even if your projections are off the mark by 10 or even as much as 20 percent, using reasonable assumptions is still preferable to not completing a hazard assessment and continuing the planning process in an information vacuum.

Mapping the Supply Chain

Successfully managing supply chain hazards requires a complete examination, analysis, and understanding of your full supply chain, both internal and external. It is critical to develop an in-depth understanding of the process flow of both goods and services. Take advantage of both your own experience and knowledge and that of other supply chain professionals in your company. An effective hazard assessment includes the insights of those who are involved in and have real-world knowledge of supply chain operations. This may be as simple as gathering all supply chain business unit managers together in a conference and together mapping the supply chain.

The Mapping Process

Developing a complete map likely requires several iterations. I suggest first creating the supply chain map on a white board to allow for additions, changes, and corrections. The representative from each business unit might use a different-colored marker to indicate his or her additions. This visual approach allows for some great what-if brainstorming while identifying all the organization's supply chain hazards.

Begin your mapping activity with the basic supply chain links as shown in Figure 5-1. Starting with your organization's facilities, add all upstream supply chain links such as tier one suppliers, contractors, and business partners, and their suppliers and contractors. Then add the downstream links such as distributors, wholesalers, retailers, and your customers. From there, create a map of the entire supply chain process and its logistics from end to end, internal and external, and all touch points upstream and downstream. Include suppliers, outsourcing, strategic partners, internal processes, shippers, customs brokers, and your customers. Once the basic mapping is complete, identify each strategic raw material and essential part or component at each upstream link of the chain. For each key supplier or contractor, list what it provides. Note if each is a sole source supplier and if not, what percentage of the overall amount required each provides. Also identify all tier two suppliers and contractors. For customers, identify what products or services you supply to each and what percentage of your overall annual sales that represents.

The supply chain map—a form of expanded flow chart— is a particularly helpful approach when a group of people are developing the hazard assessment. Each person can more quickly understand the visual representation and add his or her input. In larger, more complex organizations, this approach will likely uncover some misperceptions and gaps in understanding how each business unit fits in the bigger picture. This approach also

FIGURE 5-1.

SUPPLY CHAIN MAP.

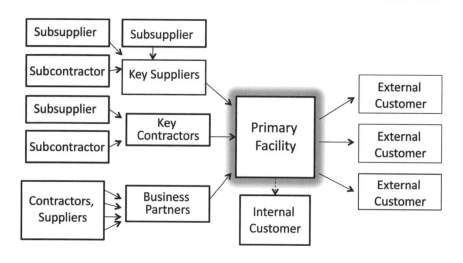

makes it possible to more readily identify the interdependencies within the supply chain.

Once the supply chain has been mapped, identify all the things that can go wrong that will prevent delivering the company's product or service within acceptable parameters. Two of the approaches for completing this task are the what-if and the checklist methods. Using the what-if approach, conduct a discussion or brainstorming session to identify what could go wrong at each juncture of the supply chain and what the consequences would be. The checklist approach involves working with a list of hazards and identifying those on the list that are threats to your supply chain This exercise will likely bring to mind other threats that are not on the list. A combination of the two may be even more effective. Use a list of known hazards as a starting point, and branch out from there to capture hazards that may be unique to your operations and location. (Appendix B contains a partial list of general hazards and a list of supply chain–specific risks to help you begin the hazard assessment process.)

Next, identify all potential disasters and unacceptable

risks. This should include all potential bottlenecks, weak links, single points of failure, choke points, and roadblocks. Then, for each of the listed threats, answer three questions:

1. How likely is it that the threat will occur?
2. Has it happened in the past?
3. If it does occur, what will the impact be on our operations?

Once this process is complete, a computerized version of the detailed map can be created for all to reference throughout the planning process. In cases where a supply chain map has never been developed before, its uses are many and go well beyond the hazard assessment process.

When reviewing a completed supply chain map, the very use of the term "supply chain" seems open to discussion. Looking at all the complex ins and outs, tiers, and dependencies, we may wonder if what we are really dealing with is actually not a supply chain but a business network or a supply chain maze or web. This visual description of the supply chain can lead to a more accurate and common understanding of the complexities of the supply chain for those who develop the map, as well as for others across supply chain functions and throughout the enterprise.

Quantifying Identified Risks

Once all possible hazards are listed, they must be quantified to prioritize the need to mitigate against and manage them. There are many ways to analyze the identified risks. For example, the risks can be graphed. (See Figure 3-2.) Another tool is the hazard assessment matrix, shown in Figure 5-2. This is a similar approach that quantifies each hazard based on two factors: the probability it will occur and the impact it will have should it occur.

For example, for a company located near a fault line in the San Francisco Bay Area, the probability of experiencing an earthquake of 5.0 or greater on the Richter scale might be rated

FIGURE 5-2.

HAZARD ASSESSMENT MATRIX.

Likelihood	Impact				
	1 Negligible	*2* Minor	*3* Moderate	*4* Major	*5* Catastrophic
5 Recurring	Low	Medium	High	Critical	Critical
4 Certain	Very Low	Low	Medium	High	Critical
3 Probable	Very Low	Low	Medium	Medium	High
2 Possible	Very Low	Very Low	Low	Low	Medium
1 Unlikely	Insignificant	Very Low	Very Low	Very Low	Low

as a probability of 3–probable with an impact of 5–catastrophic, based on factors such as exact location and the seismic rating of the company's buildings. This combination of probability and impact indicates a high level of risk requiring that mitigation measures and plans be implemented to manage the threat.

A similar way to classify threats is to put them in categories based on the level of risk it is determined each represents. For example:

→ *Level 1 Risk.* One that is limited in scope and impact

→ *Level 2 Risk.* One that is moderate in scope and impact

→ *Level 3 Risk.* One that is catastrophic, widespread in scope with long-term consequences

Applying this approach, Level 3 risks become the primary focus of mitigation and planning efforts, then Level 2, and finally Level 1 as deemed necessary.

Still another approach to analyzing vulnerabilities involves a point system. Each identified threat is scored based on five factors. Four of these use a scale of 5 to 1, with 5 being the highest and 1 the lowest. The four factors are:

1. Probability of occurrence
2. Impact on people

3. Impact on facilities and equipment

4. Impact on operations

A fifth score from 1 to 5 is given to the resources currently in place to respond to and recover from the threat should it become a reality. To score existing resources, 5 indicates that current resources are insufficient, while 1 indicates that resources currently in place are sufficient.

The five scores are totaled for each listed threat. Those with the highest scores are the ones that get the most immediate attention in the form of mitigation and planning.

Again using the San Francisco Bay Area earthquake threat example, the probability of a 5.0 or greater earthquake impacting the company is likely 3, the impact on people should an earthquake occur is 4, the impact on facilities and equipment 4, the impact on operations 4. The available resources score can vary greatly. Let's say the company has secured all office furniture, shelving, and equipment, the building is built to earthquake-resistant standards, there are trained employee response teams, a mature business continuity program in place, and redundant operations at another company location. Based on these resources, the fifth score is 2. Using this methodology, the total score for an earthquake event is 17 out of a possible 25 points.

Once the potential threats to continued operations are identified and quantified, an assessment is made of the short-term, mid-term, and long-term effects of the identified hazards on operations. This is done by using a *scenario* as a planning tool. A scenario is a brief narrative describing the hypothetical situation and conditions and the likely future when a destructive or disruptive event occurs. Based on the results of the hazard assessment, select an identified hazard and begin the process of considering the what-ifs should the disaster actually occur. Then, discuss the impact the disaster would have on your facilities, employees, and operations, as well as whether there would be supply chain interruptions and the possibility of delays in meeting customers' requirements. Using planning scenarios goes well beyond simply identifying risks and delves into the effects a given disaster would have on the organization.

Avoiding Inherited Risks

Risks can be inherited from suppliers, contractors, and the companies to which we outsource. In the past, cost and quality were the primary deciding points in selecting these important partners. With today's trend of fewer suppliers, each becomes more important, and the ability of each to meet customer requirements is increasingly vital.

To avoid the possibility of taking on unwanted inherited risks, it is essential to add consideration of the ability of these external suppliers to continue to meet obligations when faced with a disaster. While there may be a misconception that outsourcing transfers risk, the actuality is that outsourcing brings inherited risks and results in less direct control of managing those risks. Consider the unplanned loss of the services provided by a company to which you outsource and the accompanying impact on your company should there be a complete or partial loss of these services. If the service provider is a sole source provider—a single point of failure—then the potential is a total loss of critical service. If the provider has no business continuity plan and you have no contingencies for temporarily filling the gap internally and no alternate provider, then the potential risks are great and require action.

The level of scrutiny given to each of these companies is determined by the criticality of each company's input to your processes and how easy or difficult it may be to replace the supplier, vendor, outsourcer, or service provider should it be necessary. Trite but true: A chain involving a maze of business partners, service providers, third-party suppliers, and customers is only as strong as its weakest link, particularly when we are at the mercy of a sole source provider. Managing continuity risks in the supply chain is a process that inevitably involves working with these third parties to plan, execute, and monitor continuity strategies. Responsibility for supplier evaluation and selection is generally managed by the purchasing/procurement function. (This is discussed in Chapter 7.)

Applying the Hazard Assessment to Develop a Mitigation Program

Once hazards are identified and quantified to prioritize the greatest risks, a determination is made as to how best to manage, or mitigate, each risk. One of the four elements of a comprehensive business continuity program, *mitigation* is the ongoing actions taken in advance of a destructive or disruptive event to reduce, avoid, or protect against its impacts. Three choices for proactively managing any risk are:

1. Mitigate the risk by some means, such as contracting with alternative suppliers or developing alternate freight routing plans.
2. Transfer the risk to someone else, such as an insurance company, by adding or increasing insurance coverage.
3. Accept the risk by making a proactive decision to absorb any resulting financial losses.

A fourth alternative, though one that is not recommended, is to simply ignore the risk and hope it will go away. While this is an option, the reality is that left uncontrolled, supply chain risks threaten a company's financial health and brand reputation and can result in a loss of sales and—even more damaging—a loss of customers, resulting in long-term damage to the organization and its success.

Creating a Solid Foundation for Business Continuity Planning

While it is not possible to anticipate or predict all potential disasters or the full impact a catastrophic event can have on an organization, a hazard assessment is critical and has a significant effect on the ultimate success of business continuity planning efforts. Identifying all commonly considered threats and those that are unique to your company, together with the probability of each actually occurring, goes beyond simply considering disasters in the classic sense. The process gives full consideration to operational risks including those found in all segments of the supply chain. Equally important is the role of a hazard assessment in gaining an in-depth understanding of the magnitude of the disruption each threat can have on all areas of the business and the resulting ability to meet customer needs.

This quantitative, documented approach to analyzing risk leads to better informed continuity planning decisions and provides guidance for where best to focus mitigation and planning efforts and funding.

The hazard assessment combined with a business impact analysis provides a solid foundation for building a successful business continuity program tailored to the specific needs of the organization.

Going Forward

A hazard assessment is an invaluable tool in developing a program for protecting an organization and its supply chain against risk. Gaining a thorough understanding of the vulnerabilities and the related impact to the business provides information necessary for implementing appropriate mitigation strategies and lays the groundwork for the development of a valuable and realistic business continuity program.

→ If a hazard assessment was previously conducted, determine whether supply chain–specific risks were included in the process.

→ Conduct a hazard assessment of the supply chain. Involve representatives of all supply chain business units.

→ Link the results to the company's ability to produce and deliver its product or service.

→ Identify possible low-cost mitigation measures that can be implemented immediately.

CHAPTER 6

The Business Impact Analysis

A BUSINESS IMPACT ANALYSIS (BIA) is the backbone of the continuity planning process. A BIA establishes the goals to be achieved to enable an organization to continue or resume operations following a disaster. It is a tool that assists in identifying, understanding, and prioritizing the critical business functions of each business unit and the related time frame in which each must be restored to avoid the organization reaching its threshold of operational pain when disaster strikes.

The primary goal of a BIA is to separate time-critical business functions. It differentiates those functions that are absolutely necessary, either immediately or within a short time frame, for the organization to function at an acceptable level, from those functions that sustain the business and allow it to operate more smoothly and perhaps more efficiently, yet are not immediately essential to core operations. Upon completion of the analysis, some organizations find that as few as 20 to 30 percent of all business functions are critical immediately following a disaster or major disruption, while some others can be delayed for as long as thirty days—or even longer.

Once the most to least critical business functions throughout the organization are identified and prioritized, a *recovery time objective* (RTO) and a *recovery point objective* (RPO) are then assigned to each. The RTO is the target time in which the function must be operational following a disruption. The RPO is the point in time to which systems and data must be restored after an unplanned outage. Related staffing and resource needs for critical functions are also identified. From this solid foundation, it is possible to begin developing effective business continuity strategies.

The BIA: The Foundation of Business Continuity Planning

While the hazard assessment identifies and ranks potential disasters by likelihood and the resulting impact and provides guidance for prioritizing the need for mitigation, the BIA identifies the most time-critical business functions, the related necessary resources, and target time frames for restoring operations following a disaster.

I am often asked which should come first—the hazard assessment or the business impact analysis? (This is like the chicken-or-the-egg question.) If there are sufficient resources, the two processes can be conducted simultaneously. Otherwise, it's best to do the hazard assessment first, identifying and ranking the risks to your facility and operations to determine which to address most vigorously with mitigation and planning. Then, move forward with the BIA.

Another frequent question is whether it is absolutely necessary to conduct both, or either. The answer is the former: You must do both. The hazard assessment identifies the risks and operational disruptions for which we must plan, while the BIA identifies the most critical functions as well as the time frame in which they must be made operational. Omitting a hazard assessment would require the organization to prepare to manage each and every known risk at its most severe and damaging level. But without a BIA to provide matter-of-fact guidance on the priority order of restoration of business functions, the planning process would be based on the need to restore all business functions fully, immediately, and simultaneously—an approach that is neither realistic nor financially feasible.

Moreover, beyond its principal continuity planning purpose, the BIA is a valuable resource for gaining greater insight into operations across the enterprise. Upon completion, it is highly likely that the information gathered will provide a more complete and in-depth view of the entire enterprise, its operations, and internal and external interdependencies than was previously available from any single source.

Conducting the Business Impact Analysis

Conducting the BIA can seem like a nearly insurmountable challenge when first tackled. The larger the organization, the greater the effort required to conduct the BIA. The complexity of the process is further complicated when the organization has a number of geographically diverse locations or delivers several different products or services. Getting your arms around a complex international corporation or a nontraditional matrix organization is much more challenging than analyzing the operations of a small to midsize company with one location or one with a more vertical supply chain. However, the rewards are worth the effort. This comprehensive understanding of the business provides the knowledge necessary to successfully reconstitute operations following a disruption, regardless of its magnitude.

Approaching the BIA as a Step-by-Step Process

Like the proverbial elephant sandwich, the BIA is less daunting when approached as a step-by-step process. The steps are as follows:

→ *Step 1: Establish criteria for identifying time-critical functions.* This becomes the yardstick against which all business functions are measured to determine the level of criticality of each.

→ *Step 2: Decide on the data gathering process to be used, and develop the necessary instruments.* Use the method that works best for your organization, such as an electronic survey, a paper survey, a workshop, interviews, or a combination of two or more of these.

→ *Step 3: Provide orientation for those involved from whom you will be requesting information.* Let people know the reason you are requesting the information and how it will be used. This helps you overcome the challenge of making sure the information collected is complete and accurate.

→ *Step 4: Conduct the data gathering process.* Expect that it will be necessary to follow up with those who are less timely in their responses.

→ *Step 5: Review survey responses and, as necessary, conduct follow-up interviews.* Validate the information received, correct inaccuracies, clarify inconsistencies, and eliminate information gaps.

→ *Step 6: Integrate the data gathered from all business units into a single criticality order list of functions.* Establish the probable sequence in which each critical function must be restored, from most time-critical to least time-critical.

→ *Step 7: Cross-check results for all as yet unidentified internal and external interdependencies and interfaces, and adjust the criticality sequence as necessary.* A task not seen as time-critical by the business unit that performs it may have greater criticality based on how it is utilized by another business unit.

→ *Step 8: Identify the resources needed for each time-critical function.* This includes standard and nonstandard equipment, office supplies, hardware, and software.

→ *Step 9: Based on criticality, determine the maximum allowable downtime for each function.* Establish the sequence in which each critical function must be restored.

→ *Step 10: Set the RTO and RPO.* The RTO establishes a goal for the period of time within which each time-critical function will be operational following a disruption, while the

RPO identifies the point in time to which systems and data must be restored after an unplanned outage.

→ *Step 11: Report BIA results to executive management for review and, as necessary, revise the results based on management's input.* Expect that adjustments will be requested in some findings, such as priority order of restoration of some functions, based on upper management's knowledge and broader perspective of the organization and its current and future operations.

Deciding where in the organization to start can be a challenge. In a best practice approach, a BIA is conducted from the top down, starting at the headquarters or corporate level, then moving to the division or location level, and then to the individual business units in the division or location. For each business unit, you must identify the critical products and functions, measure the length of time the identified critical processes can be down without resulting in a significant delivery interruption, and determine the resources needed to support the identified functions.

Defining Time-Critical Functions

In beginning the discussion of identifying critical functions, I would like to offer an editorial comment. While most current resources for business continuity best practices use the terms "critical" or "essential," I prefer to use the term "time-critical," though "time-sensitive" would also work. I have found this works for two primary reasons.

First, put yourself in the shoes of business unit managers who are asked to assist in identifying the critical functions performed by their departments. It is likely and understandable that you would be reluctant to categorize any of the work done in your department as critical, fearing doing so would imply that any work not specifically identified as critical is unnecessary. Doing so might be construed as identifying everything else done in the business unit as noncritical. As you might expect, many managers are extremely uncomfortable going on record as having said that any of the department's work or the people who do the work are not essential. In the continuing push to accomplish more with less, you would be justified to wonder whether a secondary purpose—or perhaps even the primary purpose—of this process might be to reduce the number of positions in the department or to further reduce the budget.

Second, if a function or task is identified as not being essential, it is reasonable to question whether it is needed at all and why people are being paid to carry out these *nonessential* tasks. Managers need to be assured that the goal of the process is not to identify less critical functions with an ultimate goal of cutting positions or department budgets. Every position and every function is necessary. Managers must be told that the results of a BIA provide a rank order of all functions across the enterprise based on time-criticality. It identifies those functions that must be continued or restored most quickly following a disaster-caused interruption, as well as those that can be delayed for varying lengths of time. Its purpose is not to judge any function as being expendable but to determine how long the organization can be without each function before there is resulting financial loss, an inability to meet stakeholder requirements, damage to the brand, or failure to meet regulatory requirements.

The initial step in the BIA is to establish the criteria for determining which functions are the most to the least time-critical. Using two factors—core business and mission—it is possible to accurately define considerations to apply in determining the level of time-criticality of each of the organization's individual functions (processes or tasks).

While time-critical business functions are those that allow the organization to conduct business and fulfill its mission, equally critical are those functions that protect the organization's greatest asset—its employees—as well as functions directly affecting cash flow and those necessary to meet legal or regulatory requirements. The criteria must be specific to the organization. For instance, criteria for companies that rely on cutting-edge technology or the newest innovative product idea to give them a competitive edge will rank design or research and development functions as highly time-critical.

Organizations may also opt to identify time-critical functions as those in business units responsible for the most income or the greatest profit. Retaining customers and market share are the priorities. Since a major disruption to the supply chain can have a lasting impact on a company's ability to produce and deliver its product or service, most would agree that there is a direct correlation between an uninterrupted supply chain and income, profit, and the organization's financial picture—and in the case of publicly traded companies, shareholder value. Some companies decide that as long as the company is able to produce and ship product to the end customer, other functions (such as invoicing and tracking market trends) can wait.

Yet, because of the interrelated symbiotic nature among all business units within an organization, it is difficult to conclude that all functions performed by one business unit are highly time-critical while none of the functions of another unit are. Determining the cost of a cessation of any business function may present a challenge involving complex calculations of identifiable costs. Other costs are intangible and difficult, if not impossible, to calculate, and the greater cost may not be measurable in monetary terms but rather in terms of lost business, damage to reputation, or damage to the trust and confidence all stakeholders have in the organization. If it is possible to roughly calculate the costs for a short given period of time—say, a week—the ability to calculate the losses for five weeks is not as simple as multiplying the losses for one week times five. In the case of an extended disruption to operations, the resulting loss of customers is perhaps the greatest and longest-term damage. If your organization *is* the supplier or service provider, the BIA must take into account your post-disaster capability to continue to meet customers' needs when a disaster strikes.

Figure 6-1 presents an overview of some of the factors to

FIGURE 6-1.

CALCULATING THE COST OF DISASTER-RELATED INTERRUPTIONS.

Disaster-Related Loss	*Calculating the Cost*
Employee Productivity	Number of employees affected × hours of downtime × fully-burdened hourly rate (hourly wage plus all benefits, taxes, etc.)
Revenue	Direct loss of revenue Billing losses Lost future revenue Investment losses
Financial Performance	Cash flow Lost discounts on accounts payable Credit rating
Related Expenses	Lost or dated inventory Marketing costs Space/equipment rental Extra shipping costs Travel expense Overtime costs/temporary employees Chargebacks for late deliveries
Damage to Reputation and Trust (Intangible)	Brand damage Customer confidence Suppliers Banks and other financial institutions Stockholders
Regulatory and Legal	Fines Penalties Legal fees
Lost Customers	Inestimable losses

take into account when attempting to accurately calculate the cost of disaster-related disruptions.

Once the criteria have been developed and management has agreed that they are correct, the criticality criteria become the yardstick against which every function within the organization is measured. This provides an objective standard and helps avoid disagreements and the possibility of seeming favoritism during the BIA process.

Identifying and Prioritizing Critical Elements of the Supply Chain

While the level of criticality of functions performed within each department varies from extremely high to very low, no single department can single-handedly keep the supply chain functioning. Every enterprise has a supply chain, and within it there are products and services where disruption to supply would have a huge impact on business continuity. Similarly, most companies have major customers whose needs they must prioritize during recovery from an incident.

For supply management operations, a BIA includes a review of manufacturing, transportation, distribution services, supporting technology, warehouses, procurement, service centers, and any other business units that are directly involved in the internal supply chain. For each critical business function, it is equally important to identify the dependencies such as outsourced service providers; critical suppliers of raw materials, components, or parts; as well as critical infrastructure providers for water, electrical power, telecommunications, and all other third-party companies upon which the business function relies but does not directly control.

An uncomplicated way to measure the level of criticality of supply chain business units is to develop a series of statements that can be responded to with a *yes* or *no*. For example:

- → Function involves direct contact with customers.
- → Function involves direct contact with suppliers, contractors, or shippers.
- → Loss of function would directly result in a loss of revenue and profit.
- → Loss of function would result in loss of customers.
- → Loss of function would result in increased operating costs.
- → Loss of function can result in accounts receivable delays.
- → Loss of function would:
    - → Delay distribution of products or service delivery.

→ Delay shipment or receipt of products.

→ Delay receipt of materials, parts, or components.

→ Negatively impact the company's current highly positive public image.

→ Result in significant liability exposure or other legal ramifications.

→ Prevent the company from meeting regulatory requirements.

→ Lead to imposition of fines or other penalties for failure to fulfill delivery clauses or meet service level agreements.

→ Result in financial penalties for late payment of accounts payable

A ratio of *yes* to *no* responses provides a preliminary indication of criticality. A function with more *yes* than *no* answers requires further investigation to quantify its precise time criticality.

The supply chain map created for use in the hazard assessment is also helpful, together with available process flowcharts. Begin the BIA process with a review of internal supply chain business units such as manufacturing, purchasing/procurement, warehousing, shipping and receiving, and quality. Also consider the interdependencies with closely linked non–supply chain departments such as research and development, marketing, finance, human resources, facilities, public relations, regulatory, and legal. It should also identify the dependencies on information processing and other technology.

When conducting a BIA for the supply chain, it is necessary to recognize both internal and external components and interdependencies. No organization can deliver its product or service independently, and there is great dependency on a complex supply chain that encompasses multiple supplies and services provided from outside the organization. In global supply chains, the configuration is far-reaching and even more complex.

The importance of all touch points, both upstream and downstream, within supply networks must be considered to effectively and completely analyze disaster impacts. Supplier issues must be considered. The single points of failure identified in the hazard assessment are choke points, and their criticality must be assessed. If a key supplier or service provider experiences a disaster, consideration must be given to how it will affect internal functions identified as being highly time-critical.

Based on the BIA results, suppliers should be ranked and prioritized according to their importance to the company's mission, their relative potential risk, and the level of ease or difficulty in replacing them. Assurance of supplier continuity capabilities is of paramount concern today. With the realization that most business processes extend beyond the boundaries of any specific company, awareness of critical supply chain interdependencies has risen sharply. It is not enough (although it is important) to simply have profiles of potential high-risk suppliers and to make good choices in the supplier selection process.

Once a service provider or supplier is identified as being highly time-critical, the need to have a strategy to address any failure to deliver also becomes highly critical. As part of the BIA process, your key suppliers and contractors should be asked about their business continuity plans. (And don't be surprised if your customers ask for information about your business continuity capability when they are evaluating current or potential suppliers or service providers.)

The supply chain is a core competency of an organization and the revenue generator for most businesses. Market share, stakeholder confidence, and the bottom line all rely on continued delivery of product or service to remain healthy. Sales can or may be lost as a result of late deliveries. While customers will not necessarily take legal action if this occurs, most contracts include penalties for failure to comply. Purchase orders are binding legal contracts, and failure to meet service level agreements can result in penalties and, even worse, lost customers. Chargebacks can be another potential consequence of late fulfillment of orders.

Designing Data Gathering Instruments

There are choices in how the data for a BIA are gathered. Most often, a survey or questionnaire is distributed. Based on what works best in your organization, the document may be electronic or paper. There is no one best BIA survey or questionnaire. Each needs to be developed and tailored to the specific organization's size, complexity, and culture. As discussed earlier, a variety of off-the-shelf software packages designed to assist with the BIA process are also available.

An organization chart may be used to ensure that no business units are overlooked as well as to identify knowledgeable individuals in each business unit who are qualified to provide accurate and complete information.

Data Gathering and Follow-Up Interviews

As stated previously, it is important that those asked to provide information understand what is needed, why it is needed, at what level of detail, and how the information will be used. It should be made clear to those completing the survey that the information they provide will not be used for staff or budget reductions. It should also be stressed that the information must be based on business operations under normal conditions, rather than in a disaster situation. BIA responses should help create a "snapshot" of usual operations. If resources permit, conducting an orientation session or a workshop for those who will be providing information is a good way to initiate the data gathering process.

The survey document should be distributed with full instructions on how to complete it, as well as clear expectations as to when the information is to be returned and to whom. Contact information should be provided as well regarding whom to call if anyone has questions while completing the survey.

Information to be gathered from each business unit includes the identification by the department manager of the most time-critical functions as measured against the established criteria and the manager's estimate of the maximum allowable downtime for each function. Then, for each of the identified functions, data may be gathered on information such as:

→ Skill sets required

→ Number of persons required to carry out the function

→ Number of persons trained and capable of performing the function

→ Whether the function is duplicated at another location, and if so, where

→ Required hardware

→ Essential applications and software used

→ Nonstandard equipment required

→ Electronic documents or databases needed, the primary source for each, and, if applicable, how often it is backed up and the backup source(s)

→ Paper documents needed, the primary source, and, if applicable, the backup source(s)

→ Key times in the business cycle, such as end of quarter, end of fiscal year, and/or end of payroll cycle

→ Internal dependencies: other business units or functions

→ Essential suppliers, contractors, outsourcing companies, and other external resources required to perform the function

→ Identified alternatives for each sole source supplier or service provider

→ An estimate of minimum requirements including space, desks, computers, phones, printers, scanners, and other office furnishings and equipment

In organizations with no current business continuity program, some departments may have unilaterally taken steps to implement continuity measures. To learn about a business unit's existing level of business continuity awareness and self-preparedness, a request can be made for *yes* or *no* responses to a series of statements, such as:

→ Written procedures are in place to continue work in the event of computer downtime.

→ Shutdown procedures are in place with specific employees assigned to carry out the procedures in the event the building must be evacuated.

→ Written procedures are in place for continuing operations if building access is denied for more than twenty-four hours for any reason.

→ Alternate sources for essential supplies, materials, equipment, and services have been identified should the primary supplier be unable to meet the department's needs.

→ The department has a tested procedure for contacting employees in the event of a disaster.

Progress in the receipt of completed BIA surveys should be monitored regularly. Those whose responses are not received as expected should get follow-ups to see how completion of the document is progressing and whether any assistance is needed.

All completed surveys should be reviewed to ensure accuracy and completeness. Additional information may be necessary. Also, responses to some questions may require clarification, validation, or more details.

Follow-up interviews can be conducted to gather any additional information needed and to clarify issues arising from survey responses. It is likely that in an interview, additional information will surface that was not included in the written survey, and a discussion provides a good venue for double-checking the results against the criticality criteria.

An additional step I've found of great value during the BIA process and beyond is to draft a summary of key points from the survey and interview. Provide the summary to each person interviewed for his or her review and revision to ensure that the summary is accurate and complete. This avoids the possibility of planning based on assumptions or inaccurate interpretation of responses.

Here is an example of a BIA department summary.

BUSINESS UNIT: RECEIVING, DISTRIBUTION, AND TICKETING

Person(s) Interviewed: Susan Jackson, Business Unit Manager

Date of Interview: September 18, 2010

KEY POINTS

Function Overview

Ms. Jackson is manager of Receiving, Distribution, and Ticketing (RDT). With a total staff of 34 people, RDT is an important element in the distribution supply chain for all brands throughout North and South America. RDT interfaces with inventory, warehousing, import/export, accounts payable, buyers, and store operations. The department handles merchandise from vendors in the United States and Europe. Specific responsibilities include correcting errors such as SKU numbers and missing PO style, creating receiver authorization for merchandise shipments, closing receiver authorization, creating tickets, picks, and putaways. Prices are set at corporate headquarters and transmitted by EDI for access by RDT. Price updates are received daily.

Department employees are crossed-trained and can process all brands. In addition, step-by-step procedures have been documented in an Excel document that is revised when any processes change. Printed copies are maintained in the manager's office.

The work done in this department is not duplicated at any other location.

Most Time-Critical Business Functions / Estimated Allowable Downtime

EDI ASN invoices	1 day
Printing of picks	1 day
Printing of price tickets	1 day
Purchase order update	1 day
E-mail/communication	1 day
Intercompany transfers	2 days
Store replenishment	1 day
Generate tickets for price events (markups, markdowns)	2 days

Other department responsibilities include updating buyers of shipments by sending ASNs via e-mail, and tracking deliveries.

Peak seasons are September and October for holiday shipping, and June and July.

Applications Needed (excluding standard Word, Excel, PowerPoint, and Outlook)

JDA	Excel "Invoice Tracking Record"— daily spreadsheet used to log and track ASNs, invoices, and other related documents

EDI
(file transfer only)

Excel "Return to Vendor (RTV)"
files—manipulates data from
Invoice Tracking files

Internet to track
shipments

E-mail is critical to our
operations

RDT Menu (Menu XYZ)

Standard Equipment Needs (estimate minimum number required)

Workspaces — 12   Fax — 2
Telephones — 10   Scanner — 1
Shared Printers — 4

Special Equipment Needs

Manual ticket guns   Monarch Ticket Printers
Tickets (6 different types)

Financial Information

Loss of this function could stop or delay shipment of product resulting in lost sales and possible chargebacks.

Notes

Receive approximately 500 Advance Shipping Notices (ASNs) daily,
up to 5,000 a week. No merchandise moves without this process.

In a typical one-week period, RDT processes 60,000 pieces for
(brand) alone. During peak seasons, overtime is required to meet
shipping and delivery time frames.

Use six types/sizes of tickets, approximately 25,000 to 35,000 daily.
Some tickets are interchangeable. A 2- to 3-week vendor lead-time
is required for ticket stock; a 6-month supply is kept on hand in the
department. The vendor holds a limited number of additional rolls
of tickets for immediate availability if needed (each roll has 2,000
tickets). In addition, while tickets are not currently purchased from
other vendors, an alternate vendor that can supply all six ticket types
has been identified.

If necessary for any reason, receipts could be recorded manually in a
log and tickets could be handwritten, though this process would be
slow and require a significant number of additional person-hours.
Styles and distribution for the warehouse could also be handwrit-

ten, though doing so would take a great deal more time. An unanswered question is whether factories and suppliers would stockpile merchandise if we couldn't receive and for how long they would do so.

These summaries provide an invaluable reference throughout the continuity planning process. When combined, they present a unique and complete view of departments throughout the organization.

Determining Resource Requirements

Survey responses are then used to develop a list or database of the resources needed to accomplish business continuity. These resources include equipment, supplies, hardware, software, databases, office furniture, telecommunications equipment, and forms necessary for the resumption of time-critical functions. Both standard and special equipment needs must be identified. While most business units throughout an organization use company standard equipment such as PCs and printers, some business units have requirements for special equipment such as Mac computers, color printers, a secure printer, a dot matrix printer, wrist scanners, ticketing guns, mail room equipment, and shredders. In a disaster situation, learning that special equipment needed to fulfill an extremely critical function is not available can prevent meeting the RTO of the immediate function and all dependent functions.

A second set of resources listed should include outsourced service providers, vendors, suppliers, and contractors that are essential to the time-critical functions.

To make certain that all supply chain resource requirements have been identified, representatives from supply chain business units should be gathered to create a list of the resources needed for each critical link. This list should include people and skills, hardware, computer applications, communications capability, equipment, and services provided by suppliers, vendors, contractors, and outsourcing companies. The supply chain map helps ensure that no required resources are omitted.

Here is a word of warning when attempting to identify *necessary* resources: Business continuity is survival mode, not business as normal. It can be difficult to narrow down the perception of what is *necessary*. As an example, in an environment where every employee has his or her own office or cubicle, desk, computer, telephone, and perhaps even a dedicated printer, scanner, and fax, it can be challenging to think in terms of employees sharing a computer and telephone, having to wait in line for a printer or fax, and working together at long tables in a very large room. Business continuity planning requires thinking in terms of what is *absolutely required* to complete critical tasks—nothing more.

When identifying necessary internal resources, employee-related continuity issues are of enormous importance for companies and especially for service delivery businesses. This may include continuing operations even when employees can't make it to their usual work location because roads and bridges are impassable or employees need to take care of their families following a natural disaster such as an earthquake that destroys or severely damages homes. While business continuity planning once put great emphasis on the protection of data, information systems, and other technology, as well as on equipment, today's business continuity practitioners agree that while technology is of tremendous importance, the greater issue is employee continuity. Computers and data or sophisticated equipment without skilled and experienced employees will not fulfill customer needs.

Also identified in the BIA process is the electronic data needed to support time-critical functions. The recovery point objective identifies the maximum amount of data an application can lose before the organization begins to suffer. The RPO is typically measured in terms of time, such as four hours or one business day. For some functions in some types of organizations, where there are great amounts of money involved in transactions every minute (such as a stock exchange), there can be no data loss. In other organizations, where the amount of data processed is less or where the data is readily available for reentry, the RPO will be greater.

Identifying and Setting the RTO for Each Time-Critical Function

The last stage of the BIA process is to establish the recovery time objectives for all identified critical business functions. Starting with the most time-critical, you must determine the maximum amount of time the function can be nonoperational before it impacts the organization negatively—before monetary losses become substantial. This becomes the recovery time objective. The RTO may be thought of as maximum allowable downtime, or "how long is too long" for the organization to be without the function.

A method of grouping and categorizing functions with similar RTOs should then be established. (See Figure 6-2 for one example of how this might be handled.)

Another approach is to group functions into three categories and assign an RTO to each category. For example:

→ *Time-Critical:* Core business operations with considerable costs related to their not being operational

→ *Necessary:* Important, but relatively simple to work around for a limited period of time without the organization incurring significant losses

→ *Non–Time-Critical:* Nice to have, but loss of function for a period of time will not result in a significant loss to the organization

FIGURE 6-2.

RECOVERY TIME OBJECTIVE CATEGORIES.

Category	RTO
Level 1	0 to 4 hours
Level 2	5 to 24 hours
Level 3	2 to 3 days
Level 4	4 days to 1 week
Level 5	8 days to 15 days
Level 6	16 days to 30 days
Level 7	More than 30 days

The Business Impact Analysis Report

Once the BIA process is completed, a report is submitted to executive management that details the entire process and findings. Based on information in the report, management can approve the business functions identified as time-critical and the related priority order and time frame for continuing or restoring each, or the criticality level and sequence for some functions may be reprioritized and the RTOs adjusted.

The BIA report should include a section that addresses the potential losses that could be experienced as a result of disaster-related downtime. In calculating the losses, include lost productivity, lost revenue, diminished financial performance, and damage to the organization's reputation. Other items that may be included are extra shipping costs, overtime costs, inventory that may be lost or become dated, and money spent on marketing campaigns that will be lost. And don't forget the intangibles. This financial information demonstrates the value of meeting the continuity requirements determined by the BIA. It also helps validate the allocation of resources and funding for the business continuity program.

As with anything going to executive management, the report should be tailored to reflect its audience. The following is an example of an outline for a detailed BIA report.

EXECUTIVE SUMMARY

SECTION I: BUSINESS IMPACT ANALYSIS (BIA) PROJECT OVERVIEW

1.1   Project Mission Statement

1.2   Project Background

1.3   Methodology and Process

SECTION 2: BUSINESS IMPACT ANALYSIS RESULTS

2.1   Time-Critical Business Functions

2.2   Recovery Time Objectives

In addition to the written report, an in-person presentation of the results provides an opportunity to respond to any questions and concerns and build continuing support for the program.

Going Forward

An effective business impact analysis identifies and examines time-critical business functions and core processes in all departments that, if interrupted, would create a severe financial or operational impact on the organization. The results are used to support development of continuity strategies and the procedures needed to enable the continuity of time-critical functions. In addition, at the conclusion of the process, the department manager will have gained an understanding of the length of time that functions within the department may not be available following a disaster. Omitting supply chain business units from the BIA prevents these units from being fully represented in the business continuity planning process and resulting plans. The omission also leaves the organization's supply chain managers in an information void with respect to what the company expects of them in the event of a disaster and what they can expect from the company.

→ Determine whether a BIA was conducted in your organization.

→ If so, understand what criteria were applied to identify the most time-critical business functions.

→ Find out whether your business unit was included in the BIA and, if so, the results.

→ Determine to what extent external dependencies were addressed in the BIA.

→ If a BIA was completed, consider whether operational changes that have been implemented since it was conducted make it necessary to revisit the BIA results.

→ In the absence of a BIA, consider conducting a BIA of the supply chain business units.

CHAPTER 7

Supply Chain Business Continuity Strategies

REGARDLESS OF HOW LARGE or small an organization is or whether a company manufactures a product or provides a service, its level of success in managing the consequences of any disaster that threatens to disrupt vital business functions depends on what it does now, before the event occurs. To a great extent, successful collaboration, both internally and between the company and the numerous links in its supply chain, determines the success of its efforts to continue or restore operations.

Following a disaster, companies striving to run lean operations may no longer have inventory or excess capacity to make up for production losses, whatever the cause. As a result, supply flow problems can rapidly domino and escalate to become a further disaster for the organization. Customers neither care what created the disruption nor want a supplier's disaster to become their problem as well. They still expect the final product or service delivered at an acceptable level of quality and at the right time and price. Supply chain continuity strategies must thus address disruptions quickly enough to avoid failing to meet customers' expectations.

Possible strategies may range from the very basic, such as contracting with low-risk business partners and taking another look at inventory levels, to the complex, such as establishing reciprocal agreements for sharing office or warehouse space, equipment, and personnel following a disaster. Strategies can even involve purchasing a supplier or creating the capability to produce a critical component internally.

It is important when considering possible strategies to balance the benefits with the costs. In most cases, strategies to meet shorter recovery time objectives (RTOs) are more costly and complex. The direct and indirect costs of the strategy being considered and whether or not it will meet the planning objectives established by the BIA must always be taken into account. Once the list of potential strategies has been narrowed down, cost estimates can then be developed. A cost-benefit analysis provides guidance as to whether the cost to implement a continuity strategy will pay sufficient dividends in the form of a quicker restoration of operations following an interruption. In addition to the financial cost, operational pluses and minuses should also be considered. The RTOs for some functions may be lengthened by executive management once the full cost of meeting the originally established time frame is known.

Throughout what can be a tedious process, the focus must remain on the goal: keeping the organization's supply chain operational by continuing or restoring the business functions identified by the BIA as most time-critical. All options should be considered. Think strategically and think outside the box. Old solutions don't always work for new problems. Business continuity requires innovative problem solving.

Devising Strategies for Managing Risks

Just as your company developed its processes rather than duplicating those of another organization or buying them off the shelf, you must devise and tailor your continuity strategies to the requirements of the company. Don't be fooled into thinking that it is possible to just use the same continuity strategies and plans as those used by another organization or that you can simply purchase one-size-fits-all generic strategies, make some minor alterations, insert your company's name, and expect them to meet the unique needs of your operation.

Partnering with the Business Continuity Manager

The role of a business continuity manager is to provide leadership, direction, and oversight to ensure successful development, implementation, and ongoing maintenance of the company's continuity program. If your organization has a continuity manager or an individual who has ongoing responsibility for enterprise-wide continuity planning, some time should be spent working with this person before beginning the strategy development process. It is important to become familiar with what is already in place, related company policies, standards, and requirements. It is crucial to collaborate with the person in charge of the continuity program to avoid working at cross-purposes, duplicating effort, or developing a planning effort that results in gaps or inadequacies.

You can ensure that the continuity strategies of your supply chain business unit will successfully integrate with those of all other departments to meet stakeholder requirements, regardless of unexpected events, by collaborating with the business continuity manager and continuity team. If supply chain business units do not yet have a seat at the planning table, request that this omission be rectified. Volunteer to get involved in business continuity planning.

Another strategy is to meet with the risk manager or a representative of the risk management department. As there likely are links between risk management and continuity planning, risk management staff will often provide valuable information or assistance. Seeking input and assistance from specialists, other departments, and consultants can also bear fruit. If there is no one in the organization who has ownership of business continuity planning, gather information and do some research and reading to prepare to begin the process working on continuity planning with colleagues in the supply chain business units.

Including Loss Prevention and Security Specialists

Loss prevention and security specialists should be included when considering strategy options. Should it be necessary to temporarily or permanently relocate operations following a disaster, these business units play a major role in ensuring that the alternate site has sufficient physical security to adequately protect all facets of the operation.

The supply chain's flow of raw materials, components, parts, and finished goods, as well as information, must be protected from both external and internal risks. Ensuring that the steps necessary to accomplish this are in place is an important planning consideration for those times when the organization is in business continuity mode.

Insurance Considerations

The organization's insurance specialist is a valuable resource to tap into during the strategy development phase in order to gain an accurate understanding of insurance coverage for supply chain interruptions. In most cases, insurance is in place to cover physical losses such as buildings, equipment, and inventory. In addition, the organization may carry business interruption insurance to cover extra expenses in the event it is necessary to conduct business at a different location because of insured damage at the original place of business. Knowing what continuity expenses business interruption coverage will—and will not—reimburse can be a deciding factor in determining the best continuity strategy for the organization.

Developing Strategy Options

When developing strategies, it is important to remember that business continuity does not mean conducting business as usual.

All possibilities should be investigated. Do not immediately adopt the first solution presented. For each situation, there are many possible approaches to consider. For example, when developing a strategy to ensure the continuing availability of a key component supplied by a sole source, options can include:

→ Doing nothing, crossing your fingers, and hoping for the best

→ Working with the supplier to develop a mutually beneficial approach

→ Establishing redundant suppliers

→ Purchasing the supplier

Begin by again gathering the supply chain managers for a series of brainstorming sessions, this time to identify options for strategies for maintaining or restoring time-critical supply chain operations. The brainstorming can be based on a disaster identified in the hazard assessment as one that is both likely to happen and that would have a severe impact on operations. Each manager can be assigned to tackle two or three of his or her unit's most time-critical functions. Present a *scenario*—a brief narrative describing a hypothetical situation and conditions and the likely future when a destructive or disruptive event occurs—in which the managers arrive at work to find that the building is surrounded by yellow caution tape. In this scenario, no one is allowed access to the building or anything inside. Public safety officials report that it will be at least three days until they can allow anyone back into the building. Then, for each function, identify:

→ How operations would be impacted by the scenario

→ Current capability to address the situation

→ How long it would take to continue or resume operations based on current capability

→ Whether this meets the identified RTO

If there is a gap between the current capability and the identified RTO, brainstorm possible strategies to bridge the gap such as:

→ Temporarily transferring responsibility for the function to another of the organization's locations

→ Temporarily moving the function and the people responsible to another of the company's locations as well as temporarily suspending non–time-critical functions at the temporary location to make the necessary space available

→ Developing redundancy by dispersing the function to one or more other company locations

→ Having arrangements in place to temporarily outsource the function

→ Building a company facility now to accommodate the function in the event of an actual future disaster that displaces the function

Strategies are a must for two dimensions of every operation: (1) plans for disasters that directly impact the organization, and (2) plans for when a link in the supply chain experiences a disruption that creates a disaster ripple effect.

To be effective, strategies should vary according to industry and the organization's product or service. For example, manufacturers might opt to have an inventory of additional parts and materials stockpiled in another location—a just-in-case supply—rather than relying solely on a just-in-time approach. Retailers may have additional product ready for immediate delivery to a store in the event in-store merchandise is damaged or destroyed. Call centers can arrange to transfer calls to another location or a backup site or to activate a virtual call center if a long-term power outage or system malfunction shuts down operations at the primary location.

There are also options for continuing functions that cross enterprise boundaries and require collaboration outside the organization, such as with contractors, suppliers, or an outsourced distribution center. When addressing a scenario in which the manufacturing plant of a supplier of a critical part is flooded, considered strategies might include partnering with the supplier to identify an alternate source or arranging for the supplier to maintain an additional supply of the product at a secondary location outside the flood plain. Other options may include having plans in place to re-engineer at a company-owned facility in order to be able to quickly produce the part internally or to work with the supplier to determine if it is possible to replace the part with an alternate product.

For a food service company that thousands of customers rely upon for bread daily, a strategy to ensure a sufficient supply of bread is simply storing enough in freezers to meet the requirements for one day in the event that daily delivery is not received, whatever the reason. This—coupled with having identified an alternate bread purveyor as a backup—covers both short- and longer-term supply interruptions.

When planning for continuity in the event a disaster severely damages or destroys a production facility, dual objectives must be met. Strategies are needed to replace the output of the impacted facility and thus continue to meet customer expectations. Equally important is having strategies and plans for quickly repairing or rebuilding the facility and making it again operational.

Several recent major disasters have shown the importance of developing a supply chain that is geographically diverse. Following Hurricane Katrina, businesses that relied only on local suppliers, contractors, and shippers found their efforts to resume operations brought to a standstill. It is imperative that continuity strategies include making certain that sources for critical goods and services will be available from several geographic areas. Having the necessary agreements in place helps ensure access to products and services that are in high demand and may be in short supply locally following a disaster that impacts the immediate and outlying areas. (An interesting exercise is to locate key business partners on a map to identify situations where multiple suppliers can be hit by the same disaster or where the same disaster can impact your company and one or more key suppliers.)

From a pure business continuity point of view, multi-sourcing is an excellent strategy to avoid a disaster created when a sole source supplier fails to deliver. This strategy encourages competitive pricing and establishes fallback possibilities.

That being said, in today's business environment, the need to balance efficiency and redundancy is greater than ever before. An increasing number of companies have reduced the number of suppliers, shippers, or service providers they use, some by half or even more, in order to consolidate and negotiate lower prices. Other organizations have created new business units whose sole purpose is to manage company-wide procurement with a view toward even greater efficiencies and cost reductions.

Here again the need to consider both the benefits and the costs cannot be overlooked. Supply chain managers must continually make informed distinctions between the battling priorities of cost-effectiveness and efficient continuity strategies. As just one example of this push-me pull-me quandary, a supply chain manager may implement just-in-time-inventory to maximize efficiencies. But this approach eliminates the possibility of maintaining inventory levels that enable recovery time objectives. Relying on a single high-volume supplier rather than multiple suppliers is another decision that must be made while balancing cost, effectiveness, and continuity.

Consider the strategic continuity merits of giving a small percentage of total orders to a secondary supplier to establish redundancy. Keep in mind that the purpose is to have a source for a product or service in the event the primary supplier cannot meet delivery requirements. Of course, potential backup suppliers must be qualified. It is essential that the redundant provider be agile and able to respond rapidly to unpredictable changes in demand. In addition to standard supplier selection criteria when selecting a secondary supplier, consider:

→ Whether the company is currently producing at full capacity
→ The company's ability to meet increased needs
→ How quickly and easily the company can expand its capacity if called upon to do so
→ The ability of the company's supply network to support any required production increases

To ensure the availability of a critical supply or service provided by a *sole source*—that is, one company with one location—consider possible options. You might also contract with a *single source*—one company with multiple locations that fulfill your requirements. You might also have contracts with *multiple sources*—two or more suppliers each with multiple locations. As with all continuity strategy options, the value of such contracts must be weighed against the potential cost: *the benefit*, decreased risk of not receiving the required material or service, versus *the cost*, a more complex supply chain creating additional supply management challenges.

Yet another strategy combines continuity and mitigation. Establish a process to monitor your supply network for potential disruptions and disasters. Avoid disruptions that can result from a combination of a lack of supplier ownership and a lack of visibility. In the event suppliers and logistics providers have insufficient business continuity capabilities, explore the options.

Emerging risks can be identified by tracking details of supply chain incidents such as late or incomplete deliveries. Even the smallest glitches can portend future major disruptions. Be aware of patterns, particularly when problems occur more frequently or accelerate in scope.

Day-to-day real-time supply chain visibility systems can be applied to avoid a stoppage of incoming material resulting from any type of interruption. The visibility system can be used to review supply chain lines and take corrective action such as redirecting other incoming shipments to avoid shortages. Even with the increasing trend toward supply chain transparency, there can still be "black holes," where shipments seemingly drop off the edge of the earth for a time. Investigate what's going on in those transparency lapses to improve the ability to head off a supplier disaster.

When suppliers are not disaster-resilient, companies must find new business partners or diversify beyond their usual sources. Should it be determined that the best interests of the company are to change suppliers, contractors, transporters, or other service providers, again, the benefits of doing so need to be reviewed and measured against the possible additional costs that may be incurred. Remember, too, that there is always some level of risk involved in making such a change. Ensure that all possible steps have been taken to reduce the risks connected with the current supplier. Consider whether this is the best time to make a change in suppliers. If you decide to do so, write detailed procedures to provide to new suppliers and transporters to help ease the transition.

Plans for actions to prepare for natural disasters should be created as well. For example, for facilities located in a flood-prone area, develop strategies for reducing inventories, redirecting shipments, elevating equipment, and systematically suspending operations before flood waters are at the doorstep.

Another strategy for consideration is entering into *reciprocal agreements*, which are formal agreements made by two or more companies or organizations to use each other's resources following a disaster. These agreements, often applied to the sharing of computer and technology resources, can also be applied to other resources such as facilities, equipment, processing capabilities, raw materials and components, or employee skills.

As an example, imagine that the corporate headquarters of two companies that both produce and distribute computer software are located within thirty miles of one another. Company A's product is computer games, while Company B develops and distributes a financial software package used by small businesses. Company A has a second facility located thirty miles to the north, where its product is duplicated, packaged, warehoused, and shipped to brick-and-mortar and online retailers. Company B has a similar facility located thirty miles to the south that houses functions that are identical to those performed at Company A's second facility. Both companies use the same duplication and packaging equipment, operate on an 8:00 A.M. to 5:00 P.M. Monday through Friday schedule, and have excess warehouse space. After testing compatibility, the companies enter into a reciprocal agreement that provides for the temporary use of the other's facility and equipment should its own location be destroyed, be severely damaged, or be inaccessible for any reason for more than three days. Under the agreement, the affected company would use the other's facilities from 6:00 P.M. Friday until 6:00 A.M. Monday to run 24/7 operations over the weekend and thereby avoid a total shutdown of production and shipping. Each company now has a backup facility without the cost of building or leasing and maintaining a second location. This arrangement can work because the companies have similar products yet do not compete with one another, are in reasonable proximity of one another, and have comparable equipment.

While this mutually beneficial cost-effective strategy can be successful in some cases, care should be taken with reciprocal agreements. For one thing, you should avoid establishing agreements with other organizations that are likely to be affected by the same disaster as your company. In addition, in some cases, agreements are just not practical. For example, it is not likely that upper management would approve a reciprocal agreement with a direct competitor. There are other factors to consider. Ongoing communication between the parties is a must since changes made by one of the companies can result in it no longer being possible to exchange the agreed-upon resources. It is essential that agreements include very specific provisions defining the resources included, requirements for reporting changes in equipment or processes covered by the agreement, any expected compensation related to the use of resources, and a process for activating the agreement. Work with security and loss prevention to fully consider the potential for physical or data security breaches, and as with any other legal agreement, consult with legal counsel before finalizing the agreement.

The Devil Is in the Details

Once basic strategies are identified, dig into all related requirements for ensuring continuous business flow such as inventory levels, restocking plans, and the movement of materials, components, and parts and products. Don't forget to consider the need for skilled people to carry out the strategies.

Each department has responsibility for developing, maintaining, and carrying out business continuity strategies. While supply chain managers focus on planning for their business units, it is essential that all plans throughout the organization are fully coordinated and adhere to all business continuity policies, guidelines, and requirements established by upper-level management. A silo approach to developing strategies will result in plans that are based on incorrect assumptions and expectations and are likely to create chaos and even additional disasters when activated.

Throughout the development process, keep in mind the goal: to protect the organization by ensuring that operations can continue or be restored to an acceptable level within a predetermined time frame.

Identifying Critical Suppliers

In the early 1900s, Italian economist Vilfredo Pareto created a mathematical formula to describe the unequal distribution of wealth in his country: 20 percent of the people owned 80 percent of the wealth. Today, the Pareto Principle (also called the 80-20 Rule) has a wide range of business applications, such as:

→ 20 percent of a company's stock takes up 80 percent of its warehouse space

→ 80 percent of sales comes from 20 percent of the sales force

→ 20 percent of an organization's staff causes 80 percent of its problems

→ 20 percent of an organization's staff provides 80 percent of its production

→ 20 percent of the risks to an organization result in 80 percent of its disasters

Yet another application of this principle tells us that 80 percent of a company's materials, supplies, and parts come from 20 percent of its suppliers. If this is the case, the 20 percent become *critical suppliers*, also referred to as *survival suppliers*.

In keeping with the 80-20 Rule, it's also possible that 20 percent of your suppliers are responsible for 80 percent of your problems and can become your weakest links. An interesting exercise would be to determine if the 20 percent that are critical suppliers are the same 20 percent that create the majority of the problems.

If that is true, having continuity plans to respond to any disruption involving that 20 percent becomes an immediate priority.

You should identify your critical suppliers—those that provide essential mission-critical supplies, parts, services, or outsourced processes. The current level of satisfaction with these business partners should be examined on an ongoing basis, such as whether they have sufficient plans in place for continuing operations when disasters occur.

By their very nature, *niche suppliers* likely belong in the critical supplier category. Niche suppliers are those that specialize in providing a particular type of product or service not available from a great many providers. It is often the case that their products or services are being used by a number of different companies. If a time-critical business function is dependent on a niche supplier that is identified as a single point of failure, it is a necessity that strategies are in place to protect the company when, for any reason, the niche supply or service is unavailable from the usual source.

Reliance on critical third-party providers, suppliers, or business partners can expose the customer organization to single points of failure that both create operational disruptions and prevent resumption of operations in a timely manner. In keeping with the Pareto Principle, it would seem logical to devote 80 percent of continuity strategy development efforts to those identified as critical or survival business partners.

Testing Strategy Feasibility

Once possible strategies are identified, I suggest a reality check to be certain that the considered approach adheres to the identified recovery time objective. Start with the RTO and then subtract the time required:

→ To make all notifications
→ For people to arrive
→ To assess damage or operational impact
→ To activate strategies

→ To relocate people, equipment, and supplies, if necessary

→ To restore IT support systems and communications capability

→ To complete steps to continue or restore the function

I suggest also subtracting another 5 percent of the total RTO to accommodate Murphy, who has a way of showing up when disasters happen.

If the result of this exercise is a negative number, it's back to the drawing board to refine the identified strategy or come up with a different approach that will result in meeting the RTO.

Examining Outsourcing Options

In order to remain competitive in today's global economy, some companies have seen a need to contain supply chain costs by outsourcing supply chain and other functions. For example, in recent years there has been an increase in using third-party logistics or other services as a way to improve processes, reduce costs, or both. In this continuing outsourcing trend, no part of the supply chain—from order management to manufacturing and through to the distribution process—is exempt from risk.

At the risk of preaching to the choir, here's a reminder. Outsourcing processing and services does not transfer responsibility for quality or timely delivery to customers; it transfers only the process. While outsourcing and vendor-managed inventory and shipping can significantly boost supply chain operational efficiency, improve service levels, and reduce costs, the result leaves companies more vulnerable. The risks are still there and are possibly compounded. With critical operations managed externally, there is an increase in the number of interfaces. Operations are just not as visible on an ongoing basis, and there is a loss of direct control, leading to an increase in the number and level of risks. If not proactively managed, outsourcing may become a disaster or slow down the business continuity process when disaster strikes.

The risks in outsourcing include threats to security, availability, integrity of systems and resources, confidentiality, and regulatory compliance. When an outsourcing company performs services on behalf of your organization, increased levels of reputation risk can result. A key to successful outsourcing is to avoid putting your company's ability to meet stakeholder expectations in the hands of an organization that does not meet your business continuity standards.

List the supply chain and related business processes that your organization outsources such as distribution/logistics, warehousing, inventory control, information technology, procurement and sourcing, and reverse logistics. For each process outsourced, every possible measure must be taken to ensure that the provider is reliable, including:

→ Checking customer references

→ Auditing financial stability

→ Determining if there are inherited security risks from the outsourcing company or middlemen

→ Fully understanding what could happen and how it would impact the outsourcing company's ability to meet your requirements if that company experiences a disaster

→ Asking questions about tier two suppliers and their dependability

→ Reviewing and understanding the service provider's continuity strategies to ensure that the provider can restore services critical to your organization within time frames that are acceptable to you

→ Learning who has ongoing continuity responsibilities such as reviewing, auditing, testing, and maintaining the provider's business continuity program

Understand the impact on your organization in the event of a partial or complete loss of an outsourcing company's services. Be aware of whether the company is a single point of failure, and create continuity strategies accordingly.

Determine the advisability of developing internal manual processes to make it possible to bring the impacted operations back in house temporarily, having a redundant supplier of the service, or working with the outsourcing company to create a workable contingency solution.

Addressing Transportation Concerns

The upstream and downstream movement of material, components, and finished products—whether locally or globally and by land, rail, water, or air—is indispensable to producing a commodity and delivering it to end customers. Transportation interruptions can result from a number of causes, from frozen rivers preventing the movement of river barge traffic, to flooding or major wild land fires closing highways and railways, to labor actions such as the fifteen-day UPS strike of 1997, which caused severe disruptions to thousands of large and small companies.

Internationally, we have recently seen an example of an ancient risk reappearing to again threaten one of the world's most important shipping lanes. The continuing threat of pirates, such as those operating off the Somali coast, has serious consequences for maritime commerce. Countries including the United States depend on cargo ships for delivery of oil, petroleum, containers of dry cargo, and quantities of low-cost goods.

Yet whether the disruption is caused by something as sensational as a pirate attack or as relatively mundane as flooding shutting down a major truck route, from a supply chain perspective, a disruption is still a disruption. As a result, transportation links must be fully included in continuity planning. Whether transportation is an internal function or outsourced, and whatever the cause of the disruption, all related threats must be identified, quantified, and ranked, mitigating the risk to the extent possible, and strategies must be implemented to continue or restore receipt of upstream deliveries and distribution of downstream products.

You can ensure that strategies are in place to address transportation-related disasters by:

→ Determining whether your transportation system is sufficiently diversified

→ Developing redundancy by using multiple carriers on an ongoing basis

→ Creating strategies to implement in the event a disaster hits a transportation supplier

→ Identifying alternate routes for both incoming and outgoing shipments

The same level of attention needs to be given to the continuity planning of shipping companies as is given to all other suppliers and outsourcing companies.

The Role of Purchasing and Procurement in Continuity Planning

The purchasing/procurement department has multiple business continuity roles. The first is to develop strategies and plans for continuing the department's most time-critical functions following any interruption. The second is to develop and carry out a rigorous process that results in the selection of supply chain partners that are capable of supporting the organization's continuity strategies and that have developed an acceptable internal business continuity capability. Equally important is to take proactive steps that make possible the rapid acquisition of services, equipment, and supplies necessary to continue or quickly restore operations when disaster strikes.

Supplier Selection

Not all suppliers are created equal, and the importance of the business unit responsible for the preventive selection of suppliers cannot be overstated. Whether ultimate responsibility lies with a chief purchasing or procurement officer (CPO), a procurement team, or purchasing department staff, or whether the responsibility is managed within individual business units, the overriding goal is to select suppliers, contractors, and outsourcing companies that contribute to the goals and strategies of the contracting organization, which includes their ability to support a company's business continuity objectives.

Considerations in assessing each supplier in order to better understand the company and its importance to your organization can include:

→ Whether the supplier is a single or sole source for a vital product or service

→ The product(s) or service(s) the supplier supplies or supports

→ The level of criticality of the product(s) or service(s) the supplier provides

→ Whether your organization is considered a priority customer

→ The proximity of the supplier to your facility

→ The possibility that your company and the supplier can both be impacted by the same disaster

→ Whether the supplier's operations are geographically dispersed

→ How often the supplier's product is delivered

→ The inventory level of the supplier's product(s) typically maintained at your facility

→ The length of time required to process the order and receive the product once an order is placed with the supplier

→ The supplier's history and reputation

→ The expected level of difficulty in finding an alternate supplier

In addition, the financial health of the supplier is tremendously important in a volatile economic climate. Be sure to request third-party validation of the company's financial health and operational history. Companies that may previously have been financially sound may experience sudden and extreme financial setbacks that may result in bankruptcy or shutdown.

Significant attention should also be focused on components and services required by time-critical business functions. Rather than looking only at volume supplied or frequency of orders placed and fulfilled, the best indicator of how critical a supplier is to the organization is its role in enabling a time-critical business function to operate as intended on a day-to-day basis and to support the ability to meet the RTO when disaster strikes. Think in terms of making risk-wise selections.

Child-produced products and other unfair labor practices, hazardous waste spills, substandard and unsafe products, bribery in securing contracts, and failure to meet regulatory requirements are just a few examples of unethical business practices that are all too often in the news. When a supplier, outsourcing company, or other business partner is guilty of unethical behavior, we have an inherited business risk. We are, after all, known by the company we keep.

The risks of an ethical misconduct disaster have never been greater because of the complexity of the global business environment. Legal systems, customs, and business practices vary throughout the world, and when operating globally, it is important to understand the variations and how they conflict with your organization's positive core values, standards, and expectations.

The potential risk of a supplier's misconduct leading to an operations disruption, harm to your organization's financial performance, loss of public trust, and a media feeding frenzy can and should be mitigated. Avoid inheriting reputational disasters by factoring into the selection process a supplier's ethical principles and standards of conduct. Educate your supply chain partners. Familiarize every current and potential supplier and outsourcing company with your organization's code of ethics and conduct. Make them aware that you conduct supply chain management in accordance with national and international laws, customs, and practices, as well as your internal policies, ethical principles, and standards of conduct. Enact a no-tolerance policy regarding unethical or illegal business practices. Contract with businesses that hold the same high standards as your organization and that manage their social and environmental impacts responsibly. As part of the selection process, ask those vying for your business to provide their code of ethical conduct that outlines their health and safety, labor, environmental, and business integrity standards. In your vetting process, check for any history of unsavory business practices or hint of scandal.

Apply your code to your direct suppliers, and let them know that your expectation is that they will ensure that their upstream suppliers adhere to the same high ethical standards.

Equally import is to be certain that your suppliers walk their talk by demonstrating business practices that match the published code. Conduct periodic ethical audits to ensure that outsourcing companies are adhering to your expectations. Monitor their actions. Let each link in your supply chain know that any regulatory breaches or ethical misconduct will not be condoned and will be taken seriously when you are renegotiating supplier contracts. Make integrity continuity, protection of the ethical reputation of your company, a component of supply chain business continuity management by avoiding partnering with any company or person who does not adhere to your company's moral and principled standards.

While cost, quality, technological capability and compatibility, customer support, and compliance with the customer's labor practices, ethical standards, and regulatory requirements must be considered, the supplier's ability to manage its risks must not be ignored either. Seek to contract with suppliers with a mature business continuity capability.

Customer-supplier relationships are necessarily strategic. Yet despite increased outsourcing and greater reliance on suppliers, it is still not a given that the supplier's continuity capability is a factor in the selection process. Look at your supply chain from a risk management perspective. Go beyond purely financial considerations and also look at continuity capabilities. Cost savings alone may not seem as sensible if a failure on the part of a time-critical supplier or contractor results in a significant break in your supply chain.

It is important to be knowledgeable of critical suppliers' level of disaster preparedness and the steps they have taken to prepare to continue business following a disaster that impacts their operations. "We can handle it" is no longer an acceptable response to questions asked of suppliers regarding their capability to continue to meet your requirements should they experience a disaster.

It is essential to include business continuity considerations in the evaluation process when you are selecting new suppliers and reviewing current suppliers. Hearing a supplier or outsourcing company state, "We have a business continuity plan" is simply not sufficient. Even if suppliers have a business continuity plan, it is important to understand how they will support your requirements, where you fit in their continuity priorities, and how quickly they will restore service to your organization when they experience a disruption.

Continuity capabilities within the framework of your organization's requirements need to be evaluated. If metrics or benchmarking are used in the selection process, ensure that business continuity factors are fully considered in the evaluation criteria.

Beyond just knowing that a plan exists, gathering specific information allows you to gauge the level of continuity preparedness as it relates to your organization's needs. Ask each supplier, contractor, service provider, and other business partner for the following information:

→ The scope of its continuity plan—for example, whether it is a comprehensive business continuity plan or a disaster recovery plan that covers only IT

→ How long the business continuity program has been in place

→ The owner and the sponsor of the business continuity program

→ Whether the planning process included a hazard assessment and business impact analysis

→ The frequency of scheduled training and testing

→ The date the plan was last exercised or tested

→ The date the plan was last reviewed and updated

→ Whether the plan has been audited; if so, when and what were the results

→ The degree to which all employees are familiarized with the business continuity plan

→ Whether backups of vital paper and electronic records are stored off-site

→ Whether procedures are in place to continue or restore minimum service levels following a disaster

→ How your organization will be supported if the supplier experiences a serious disruption in operations and the plan is activated

→ A clear-cut time-specific definition of how long delivery of the supplier's product or service to your company would be delayed within the framework of the plan

→ Whether the company is confident that it is adequately prepared to handle all unplanned operational interruptions

Any unacceptable or ambiguous responses should be considered a red flag.

When You Are the Supplier

When the shoe is on the other foot and it is your company being evaluated as part of a selection process, having a business continuity program in place can be a marketing advantage. Expect that prospective customers will ask you for information about your business continuity capability. Consider what your responses will be when you are asked for the continuity information listed above. Be sure that your responses will meet the potential customer's requirements to avoid your company being excluded from the selection process.

In some cases, an organization may request a copy of your business continuity plan document. While I understand the need to ensure a supplier's continuity capability, I believe that there are some serious issues with turning over a copy of your plan, even to a valued customer. Continuity plan documents typically contain some highly confidential, proprietary, and sensitive information such as the names, home addresses, and telephone numbers of employees—including executives and perhaps board members—as well as business strategies, financial information, client information, process flows, and technical specifications. You thus need to avoid plans getting into the hands of a competitor, anyone who could use the information for illegal purposes, or even a terrorist.

Here are a couple of suggestions for giving a customer or potential customer the necessary information while safeguarding confidential information:

→ Provide a copy of the business continuity mission statement signed by the executive sponsor, the table of contents, the plan overview, the plan review/update record, any audits referencing business continuity, and a record of training sessions, tests, and exercises.

→ Alternatively, provide a sanitized version of the plan to be read on-site. Issue an invitation to participate in your next scheduled test or exercise, and offer to participate in theirs.

If these options are simply not acceptable and a copy of the plan must be provided, go over it with a fine-toothed comb and omit any and all sensitive, confidential, or proprietary information. Have the edited version reviewed by legal as an additional precautionary measure.

Reviewing Supplier Continuity Plans

You may be uncertain about the need to review the business continuity plans of supplier tiers. Good judgment and common sense come into play here. Tier one and possibly tier two suppliers should be included, as well as possibly tier three in lesser detail. Conducting a review of the tier suppliers' business continuity capability beyond tier three becomes superfluous.

The bottom line is to ensure that you have conducted *due diligence*—in other words, appropriate carefulness, reasonable care and attention, and the degree of care that a prudent person would exercise.

The incorporation of business continuity considerations in each step of the selection process should include interviews with management. Start with the request for proposal (RFP) and have bidders include information outlining their continuity capabilities or use the list presented previously in this chapter of requested information.

When conducting site interviews during the selection process, be aware of potential disasters, both inside the supplier's facilities as well as in the surrounding area. Notice the safety and security measures in place, particularly in geographic areas where standards are lax. To maintain operational efficiency, many suppliers have only one location. In the event a disaster such as a fire occurs in a single-location supplier plant with no sprinkler system, the entire building could be destroyed. The resulting time required to rebuild or relocate could be months or even longer, possibly leaving your organization with a fractured supply chain in the meantime.

Contracting with Suppliers

Business continuity requirements need to be included in contract negotiations. Contracts should include detailed continuity time frames that meet the continuity planning needs established by your BIA. A best practice planning process includes developing and maintaining call lists for contacting key individuals for all suppliers and other stakeholders. Contracts should specify that the contractor will make complete contact information available and make prompt notification of any changes to any of the provided contact information. Contracts should also detail how the business partner will fulfill its commitment to maintaining services should it be necessary for the supplier to operate from an alternate location.

A contract clause that requires the vendor or contractor

to develop or continue to maintain a business continuity program might also be considered.

Your legal department or legal counsel should be used to build appropriate business continuity wording into contracts and to review any contracts provided by the supplier. For instance, many construction and supply contracts contain a *force majeure* clause, which is an unanticipated or uncontrollable event or effect that releases the contractor from fulfillment of a contractual obligation. While these clauses may be acceptable in most circumstances, they may not be acceptable from a business continuity planning point of view. (Reading a force majeure provision may result in your eyes crossing and a feeling of light-headedness as you endeavor to gain a full understanding of both the legal language and the ramifications invoking a force majeure clause will have on continuity strategies.) Force majeure events are whatever the contract says they are. Depending on contract language, such events can be a hurricane, tornado, terrorism, labor action, change in ruling regime, transportation shortage, or an unending list of other events. In a global supply chain, there is always an event that is outside your supplier's control.

A last-resort strategy is to take legal action after the damage is done—when a provider fails to meet service level agreements or contract terms. While there may be some recovery of financial losses, the greater loss is likely to be both tangible, in the form of lost customers and business, and intangible, such as an effect on customer confidence, reputation, and the perception the marketplace has of your organization. A procurement process that gives consideration to a potential business partner's continuity capability is in the best interest of the organization and all its stakeholders, including supply chain partners.

As contracts come up for renewal, they should be reviewed from a continuity risk perspective. This is the time to reassess the supplier's continuity capability. Initiate discussions with the time-critical vendors regarding changes in your organization's business continuity processes and your current expectations of business partners. Let them know that your strategies rely on their level of capability, particularly in the case of single or sole source relationships. Describe your organization's current supply chain continuity requirements and identify any specific desired corrections to be made by the supplier. Make sure that contract content still serves your organization's best interests. If there is a service level agreement in place, check to see if it contains required business continuity–related provisions.

Supplier Monitoring

Too often, consideration of a supplier's level of continuity preparedness occurs during the selection stage, but ongoing monitoring is ignored. It is not enough to evaluate only the inherited level of risk a supplier brings to the contract signing. The financial and operational stability of critical suppliers needs to be measured on a regular basis as well. It is important to understand and to continue to assess the supplier's financial picture. Circumstances can shift quickly and have extremely detrimental impacts on a business. Suppliers can also inherit risks from their own business relationships that may not be obvious in an initial evaluation.

The operations of suppliers, contractors, and outsourcing companies should be regularly monitored. Track incidents, visit their facilities, and when you do, get beyond the executive offices and visit the manufacturing floor and the employee break room if possible.

Managing a global supply network is demanding, and the challenges are multiplied when there are a large number of suppliers. If tracking systems are available at all, there are often significant system disparities and the data that is available is often fragmented and inaccurate. Managing suppliers in this environment necessitates establishing requirements for consistent metrics and measurements. When the supply chain is international in scope, you should develop an understanding of global risks and be aware of political and environmental changes that impact your supply chain.

If a scorecard or other metrics is used to evaluate suppliers, it should include supply chain continuity factors such as when the continuity plan was last audited and updated, the date of the most recent tests and exercises, and the extent of employee continuity training. Used effectively, the scorecard becomes a valuable communications tool when encouraging suppliers to establish or enhance their business continuity program.

Ensuring Continuity Support in Procurement

In addition to ensuring that the organization contracts with disaster-resilient business partners, procurement business units play an important role in supporting the strategies to be employed when a disaster occurs.

These units identify specialized vendors and contractors who will carry out or support continuity strategies and make available as-needed purchase orders. Pre-identifying the companies and providing them with a purchase order or crate and ship agreement now saves valuable time and gets requests for materials and services filled before those who wait to act until the disaster happens. These agreements can make the difference between successfully meeting RTOs and experiencing serious delays. These agreements can be particularly helpful when a disaster impacts a wide area and services such as cleanup and salvage are in great demand.

Some organizations have a complex and lengthy procurement process. Consider your organization's contract and purchase approval procedure and how long it takes. Having the resiliency needed to meet continuity requirements may include developing a streamlined procurement process that can be temporarily activated as necessary in order to quickly arrange for needed supplies, equipment, and services following a disaster.

In addition, review how many signatures are needed to approve contracts and purchase orders and to sign checks, as well as the number of individuals authorized to sign these documents. Consider whether it would be beneficial to have a post-disaster policy that temporarily either decreases the number of signatures required or authorizes additional individuals to sign the documents.

Partnering with Suppliers

A relationship always exists between a customer and a supplier whether it is good, bad, or ugly. To best meet the continuity needs of both, consider working to elevate the relationship to a mutually beneficial, collaborative, integrative partnership. This entails both relationship management and supply chain management. While today's supply chains may be highly automated, business continuity does not rely on technology alone. It is through a collaborative approach—partnering with your suppliers, contractors, and shippers—that the most effective supply chain continuity strategies are generated. For some, this is a new way to look at supplier-customer relationships.

Forward-thinking organizations are following today's supplier-customer trends. These include establishing long-term relationships, having supplier management take steps to improve performance through a formal evaluation process that has as its goal mutually beneficial change, and forming strategic partnerships—trusting relationships with key suppliers. When suppliers and customers truly partner in addressing business continuity, the end result is mutually beneficial continuity strategies, a win-win for all involved.

While it can take some work to change a relationship that may have been adversarial into a cooperative one, in the long run, the dividends are well worth the effort. When developing supply chain business continuity strategies, use a cooperative approach among all those involved in your supply chain. View suppliers, domestic or international, as strategic partners. Develop and then build on good relationships with suppliers, forwarders, logistics services companies, brokers, and contractors, just as you do with your customers. Work *with* your supply chain partners.

Suppliers are stakeholders that want to have you as a customer, yet they have their own hazards and continuity requirements. Meet with time-critical suppliers and discuss your business continuity planning goals with them. When visiting key suppliers, meet with their leaders and discuss what your organization's business continuity program is all about. A non-adversarial intra-organization partnership approach to business continuity can make a positive and significant difference in how successful your organization—and partner organizations—can be in continuing or more rapidly restoring operations following a disaster. Share information and ideas. Consider not only your organization's needs but those of the partner organization.

To be effective, this approach requires that both parties are open about the risks they face. For tier one suppliers, this should include identifying threats that are inherited from tier two suppliers.

It is reasonable to assume that working with you has benefits for your suppliers. Let them know your expectations. A basic step toward accomplishing this is to include continuity readiness as a factor when awarding future contracts. True continuity partnerships require that companies collaborate directly with their suppliers. Establish business continuity performance measures and reward suppliers who consistently meet or exceed the performance indicators. Keep the lines of communication open. When suppliers fall short of the continuity performance goals, discuss performance issues promptly to provide them with an opportunity to quickly correct them. Establish a process that will lead to a cooperative approach to resolving any issues that arise. A partnership in the planning process lays the foundation for greater collaboration in developing and carrying out continuity strategies.

While it is important to convey the message that there are expectations for supplier business continuity competency, at the same time, it is also important in an overall program of customer-supplier collaboration for you to provide information, guidance, and assistance. In the event a business partner does not yet have a business continuity program, avoid an "us versus you" approach by simply dictating what they "should do." Instead, initiate an ongoing dialogue.

It can be useful to see your interest in business continuity planning from the perspective of a supplier or other business partner. While suppliers need to take responsibility for and have full ownership of their own business continuity programs, a customer requirement for such a program may be the primary driver. Put yourself in the place of suppliers whose customers are demanding that they initiate business continuity planning several months after a contract is in place. Likewise, imagine that you are a supplier and, while preparing to respond to a request for proposal or in the middle of negotiating a contract renewal with a customer, you first learn of newly added business continuity requirements. Presumably, you would not be pleased. In some cases, suppliers and contractors are much smaller than the organization they supply and have limited resources to initiate a continuity program. Help your suppliers by providing them with your requirements early on and encourage them to take responsibility for their continuity programs.

In addition, providing a reasonable amount of hands-on assistance to help suppliers develop a business continuity strategy may be worth consideration. This can include:

→ Sharing business continuity standards and policies

→ Providing sources for business continuity training

→ Presenting supplier business continuity workshops to provide them with a better understanding of your organization's continuity requirements and guidance in developing their own program

→ Offering project management assistance with the planning process, such as a project outline with a suggested timeline and milestones

→ Sharing planning templates and tools

→ Including suppliers and contractors in your business continuity training sessions and/or exercises

→ Offering business continuity planning coaching

While opting to take advantage of any offered assistance is strictly the decision of the supplier, these steps will show your organization's willingness to cooperate rather than dictate.

When a disaster occurs, prepared supply chain partners are in a better position to leverage each others' operational capabilities if realistic advance planning has been done to define mutual expectations, roles, and responsibilities, and redundant communications and information sharing tools. Partnering with your suppliers is certain to pay dividends.

Disaster Recovery: IT Support of the Supply Chain

Very few organizations have IT as their business, yet in today's business world, technology is fundamental. It has enabled business to make enormous strides and continues to allow us to conduct business more efficiently, but it is often taken for granted. Companies—both manufacturers and service providers—recognize that recovering technology alone will not restore business functions and processes. Nonetheless, technology is a critical piece of the continuity puzzle that must be included to complete the picture.

While business continuity is not a technology issue, disaster recovery *is* the technology component of business continuity and is the IT department's business continuity plan. Computer and communications systems are the center of complex procedures that underpin a wide range of business and management activities. Expanded use of the Internet and the growing reliance on e-mail has made even short-term system downtime unacceptable. Not that many years ago, upon completion of business impact analyses, e-mail was not often seen on the list of time-critical IT support functions. Today, BIA results for most organizations place e-mail at or near the top of the list of critical IT functions.

The supply chain's dependence on technology has never before been greater than it is today, creating a critical need for IT support. Advancing technology has brought about great advancement and equally great challenges. The growing reliance on receiving and viewing documentation from supply chain partners is just one example of this reliance. While the IT department may have an excellent disaster recovery plan to restore technology infrastructure, recover networks, and restore applications, supply chain IT requirements may inadvertently be overlooked or not fully considered during the development of disaster recovery strategies and plans.

This oversight may result from the lack of full inclusion of the supply chain in the business continuity process or from a bottom-up planning process driven by the technology departments and having as its goal the development of only a disaster recovery plan rather than an all-inclusive business continuity program. When planning is done from the top down, a business continuity analysis is conducted by the business continuity planning group, and disaster recovery planning is based on meeting the requirements established by the BIA.

Business continuity is an operational and staffing problem, not a technical problem, yet the dependence on technology to provide support to the critical functions and the staff performing them is omnipresent. To retain a global competitive edge, companies throughout the world that have largely automated their manufacturing operations must consider the impact of technological disruptions and disasters on those operations. The proliferation of automation that has resulted in more cost-effective and agile manufacturing has also created a greater need to have coordinated, integrated business continuity and disaster recovery plans in place.

To illustrate the reliance many companies have on technology, consider an *enterprise resource planning* (ERP) system—an integrated information system that serves all departments within an enterprise to coordinate manufacturing processes to enterprise-wide back-end processes—to manage sales and purchase elements of supply chain operations. The data stored in an ERP system (such as suppliers, customers, materials, components, and parts) and the internal process flows and control functions within the system (such as sales order entry, generation of purchase orders and invoices, inventory control, distribution, and work orders) integrates the once-fragmented end-to-end business processes throughout the entire organization. In addition, the ERP system may link to external systems or have embedded accounting functions such as payables, receivables, and general ledger entries. The reliance on the ERP technology that controls internal functions from sales orders, picking, packing, and sales commissions to inventory, distribution, invoicing, and processing of returns and chargebacks is indicative of how dependent today's supply chain operations are on technology and the importance of full inclusion of supply chain requirements in disaster recovery planning.

A fundamental disconnect often exists between IT and the other business units, creating a communications and collaboration challenge. Bridging that gap is a must when developing business continuity strategies and plans, and this requires working with the IT department's disaster recovery manager. While the IT department has chief responsibility for disaster recovery and the restoration of computer systems, data, and communications systems, it is imperative that supply chain managers provide input and feedback during the process to ensure that the resulting plan meets supply chain needs.

Those involved in business continuity planning, even if not directly involved with the workings of the organization's technology, can benefit from having a basic understanding of the technology required to continue or resume operations. Just as important, the person in charge of disaster recovery planning must be aware of time-critical functions in all business units and fully understand what technology and electronic data are needed to support the continuity of those functions and how quickly each function must be operational.

In all businesses, it is critical to gain an understanding of whether and to what degree the supply chain was considered when the disaster recovery plan was developed, what level of priority was assigned to supply chain IT support components, and the assigned RTO for each of the time-critical supply chain technical elements. This can be achieved by using the supply chain map. (See Chapter 5.) Overlay the IT functions that support and connect critical supply chain functions. Work with an IT representative to make sure that all IT support needs can be met, including the flow of information. As a supply chain professional, you are not expected to be fully knowledgeable about IT and the related technology that support your operations. What is necessary is that you and the IT professionals who are responsible for disaster recovery in support of business continuity strategies and plans fully understand the recovery needs of the supply chain and have plans in place that support those needs. This involves asking whether supply chain applications, databases, and connectivity were included in the last test and, if so, what the results of the test were, including the recovery time.

If your data backup policies, technology, and procedures are not well thought out, other aspects of disaster recovery planning are greatly diminished. Backup is the foundation of a successful disaster recovery strategy. Be aware of how often supply chain data is backed up, the technology used, how often the backups are taken off-site, and where they are stored. Ascertain whether electronic vaulting is used to immediately move data off-site to a secure location. When a disaster occurs, it is important to know how long it will take for supply chain data to be restored.

IT must be kept in the loop regarding any process changes to ensure that those changes are reflected in disaster recovery plans. Sharing knowledge between the technology and supply chain business units is critical when disaster strikes, as well as having tremendous value on a day-to-day basis.

Establishing Work-Around Procedures

A fundamental element in effective business continuity strategies is the establishment of alternative methods for operations. Whether a disaster impacts the entire organization or results in only a loss of IT support, individual departments have responsibility for planning how they will continue or resume critical operations.

Plans and procedures to cover technology outages should be part of each department's strategies. Interim procedures that may be used by a business unit to enable it to continue to perform its critical business functions during temporary unavailability of IT support systems are commonly referred to as *work-around* or *user-react* procedures. These procedures are documented in department continuity plans to provide guidance and instructions for continuing the department's most time-critical functions while interrupted IT support is restored.

Work-around procedures should be developed as part of the department planning process and are activated when the physical plant is undamaged and accessible and the data center is experiencing a major outage.

Consider whether manual processes are possible for some time-critical functions in order to allow operations to continue while electronic systems are restored. Avoid business-as-usual thinking. While work-around procedures are not usually pretty, since they are slower and necessitate that transactions still must be entered into systems once they are restored, they can prevent a full stoppage of many time-critical functions.

A situation I experienced not long ago provides a simple example of how work-around procedures can prevent a minor disruption from becoming a disaster. Arriving at the front door of a large home furnishings store one morning, I found handwritten signs on locked doors stating "Closed—our computers are down." A work-around procedure to remedy this situation would have begun with cashiers pulling out printed step-by-step procedures, receipt books, hand-held calculators, and credit card slide machines. While less efficient, this work-around would have made it possible for the store to open its doors and continue to sell product and provide customer service while the automated system was being restored. The end result is an inconvenience, rather than a disaster resulting in lost sales, lost customers, and damage to reputation and brand.

In developing department business continuity work-around procedures, an approach I've found effective is to open the discussion this way: "Our computer systems are expected to be down for three days. We need to identify *how we will* complete the tasks identified as time-critical without the use of a computer until restoration is complete." Avoid asking, "*Can* we accomplish that critical function without the computer?" The answer will most likely be, "We can't." Instead, assume at the outset that there is a way to accomplish the time-critical tasks.

Addressing Infrastructure Needs

While not necessarily under the disaster recovery umbrella, a comprehensive planning process will address the need for infrastructure to support operations as well. In today's world, we need electric power, telecommunications, water and wastewater service, and perhaps natural gas to keep our operations running. These utilities are not referred to as lifelines for no reason.

The blackout of 2003 that created a power disruption across eight states in the United States and parts of Canada was a strong yet short-lived reminder of our dependency on the utilities we often take for granted. While memories of the 2003 power outage continue to fade, smaller power outages continue to regularly occur.

A growing number of companies have installed power generators, the capacity of which ranges from powering only emergency lighting to fully powering every part of the facility. It's important to know whether your building has emergency generators and even more important to know exactly what they power and for how long. Making incorrect assumptions about what in your department is powered by the generators can have serious consequences when the lights go out. Also be aware of what equipment in each business unit has an *uninterruptible power supply* (UPS)—an alternate short-term power supply, usually battery-powered, to maintain power in the event of an electrical power outage. Power and telecommunications providers are suppliers and can be identified in the BIA as single points of failure. Since more power and telecom disruptions result from lines being dug up by backhoe operators than from terrorist attacks, it is likely that your power or telecom outage will be local in scope. Explore the feasibility of having power and telecom lines coming into your building from two different locations or having secondary suppliers.

Make no assumptions. Request that necessary adjustments be made to ensure that infrastructure services are available to support continuity or rapid restoration of time-critical functions.

Considering the Human Factor of Business Continuity Planning

An area that has recently garnered greater attention is the human factor of business continuity. Horrendous events like 9/11 forced companies to consider what would happen if employees were lost and whole buildings destroyed. While our hope is to never again experience such an event, people issues must be included when developing continuity strategies. Most human resources issues arise when a disaster results in denial of access to your facility or when people are not available to do the work. In the event your location is not accessible, have plans in place for your people regarding issues such as where they will work, who will relocate, and who will manage business continuity processes.

Recently, the potential for a widespread pandemic received a great deal of attention on local, national, and international levels with the global emergence of a new strain of the H1N1 virus (commonly and incorrectly referred to as swine flu). Media coverage kept the topic in the news as the World Health Organization (WHO) monitored the situation and advised the public of the changing worldwide pandemic alert level.

In spite of daily coverage in the broadcast and print media and warnings from health officials, it was difficult for many people and organizations to take the pandemic threat seriously. There is every indication that a majority of businesses opted not to develop formal plans for responding in the event that the global pandemic threat became a reality, or that they simply ignored the issue altogether. No historical data and information exists as to how a full-scale pandemic would impact today's business economy and day-to-day operations. However, in the event the current pandemic threat level is raised or a future pandemic threat appears on the horizon, Appendix C provides a Pandemic Planning Guide that can be used for reference—just in case.

When developing continuity strategies, fully consider the human factor—the people who keep the supply chain moving. Imagine this scenario: A disaster destroys your primary business location. Business continuity planning strategies include shifting critical operations to a nearby alternate facility, which is now open with critical equipment and IT support installed and operational. One critical factor is missing. No employees show up. Even technically sophisticated systems and equipment require people to keep operations running smoothly.

Succession planning is needed for all critical skill levels—not only for executives and senior leaders. Employees should be cross-trained to ensure coverage for all identified time-critical business functions for times when those with primary responsibility are not available. This requires initial training and ongoing hands-on practice with guidance and direction from the person who has primary responsibility for the work. In some cases, it is necessary to arrange for required certifications and licensing. Most employees appreciate the opportunity to learn new skills sets, and this helps ensure that there is backup to cover functions when those primarily responsible are not available. In addition, when in continuity mode, it may be necessary to continue operations on a 24/7 basis. Having additional qualified people provides the necessary support to make this work schedule possible.

You should create and maintain up-to-date, documented procedures that will allow backup personnel to carry out critical business functions. To the extent possible, a manual of detailed work-around procedures should be developed in the event full IT support systems are not functioning.

Encourage and assist employees in preparing their homes and families for disasters. I have read business continuity plans that call for employees to "immediately report to work" following any disaster. In the event of a widespread natural disaster, the reality is that most employees will report only once they are assured that their loved ones are taken care of. Having a family disaster plan in place enables employees to move quickly to take care of family needs and then report as assigned.

When a disaster occurs, all employees can be kept informed through the use of an employee 800 number, e-mail, the intranet, or one of the increasingly sophisticated electronic notification systems. Employees want to know about the status of the disaster and its immediate and future impacts on the organization. They need to know what they are expected to do, such as when and where to report to work or if they are to stay at home until notified otherwise, and when updated information will be available.

The Importance of Disaster Communications

Maintaining contact with employees, other company locations, customers, suppliers, contractors, regulatory agencies, shareholders, and other stakeholders—anyone essential on a day-to-day basis—is a critical element of business continuity. Often overlooked or given insufficient attention, continuity communications strategies need to be established and detailed in your business continuity plans.

Situations initially viewed as minor annoyances or small emergencies may turn into disasters if adequate stakeholder communication is not maintained. Being prepared to manage requests from print media, radio, and television can help ensure that media coverage does not become a secondary disaster as a result of not being well managed.

Identify the supply chain links with whom your company needs to communicate when a disaster occurs. Include both those who have an actual need for information and those who believe that they need information. In the case of the latter group, remember that if you don't provide information, they will most likely get it elsewhere or even "create" their own answers.

In addition to employees who want to know what they are to do and how the crisis will impact them and their jobs, it is important to have strategies in place for keeping those who may have heard about a crisis and who have a vested interest in your company in the communications loop. This includes customers who need assurance that the products or services they receive from you will still be delivered on time at the quality level they expect and suppliers who need to know of any changes to orders, delivery schedules, or delivery locations.

Effective strategies address the four components of effective disaster communications: (1) getting the right information to the right people at the right time, (2) the technical capability to communicate, (3) clearly communicating the information, and (4) rumor control to prevent misinformation.

Start with emergency communications basics:

→ Implement enterprise-wide emergency calling systems and procedures.

→ Coordinate contact processes throughout the organization to avoid duplication or omissions.

→ Standardize notification lists, and review them for accuracy and updates no less than quarterly.

→ Ensure that call notification lists include all contact information such as cell phone, text, home phone, second home phone, work e-mail, and home e-mail.

→ Make certain that call notification lists for business continuity team members include both primary and backup team members in the event primary persons are unavailable or do not respond.

→ Brand all call notification systems—calling trees through sophisticated electronic systems—with identifiable names so that the person answering the phone is immediately aware of the call's importance.

→ Include key supplier, contractor, and outsourcing company representatives in call notification processes.

→ Have multiple options for emergency notification.

Your post-disaster communication with stakeholders such as transportation companies, customers, and suppliers will be timelier and more effective if, before a crisis occurs, there is preassigned responsibility for keeping key contacts informed. Identify who will establish and, as necessary, maintain contact with whom and how. As with all others who have business continuity responsibilities, have a backup for each person who is assigned communications responsibility.

Create a database of key stakeholder contacts that is maintained and updated frequently. Present your information to all stakeholders quickly and honestly. As appropriate, provide frequent updates on how you're doing in responding to and recovering from the disaster. While they will sympathize with your plight, customers need to know how your situation impacts them, and specifically whether the service or product you provide will be delivered as scheduled.

If not already in place, consider enacting a company policy that employees are not to give any statements about the company to the media. Not everyone is skilled at giving interviews, and having a no-statement policy benefits both the organization and its employees. It protects employees from possibly being responsible for incomplete, incorrect, or proprietary information making its way to the front page of a newspaper or from being the source of a damaging sound bite on an evening news broadcast.

Also, consider how your company's Internet presence can be used to communicate your message when a crisis occurs. An additional preassigned continuity role can be a person or persons who facilitate use of the Internet to contact identified stakeholders and keep them advised of the company's actions in responding to the disruption. The role can also encompass making information available to the general public.

Educate employees about the importance of following the company's media policy and provide them with information about to whom to refer media representatives. Include complete and accurate contact information. Having a reporter with a microphone ask for your opinion or having a news camera bearing down on you can be compelling. While reporters have the right to interview anyone they want, everyone has an equal right to decline to be interviewed. Having a "no comment" policy and knowing to whom to refer media representatives provides direction and makes it easier for employees to decline to comment.

The importance cannot be overstated of making the necessary internal notifications following a disaster. To prepare for successful disaster communications, develop and regularly maintain notification lists, including immediate internal notifications to be made in each type of crisis, such as executive managers, public relations, security, human resources, and legal. Designate how each person will be contacted and by whom. Include business and home contact information such as landline telephone, cell phone, PDAs, and e-mail. In addition to laminated cards listing company emergency contact numbers carried by all employees, those with continuity responsibilities can be provided with cards listing numbers they will need when the business continuity plan is activated.

Disaster communications capabilities should be tested often. Update all contact lists and contact information in electronic notification systems. Ensure that those assigned communications responsibilities receive complete training with periodic updates and refresher training. Develop communications redundancies and test the technology on a regular basis.

Going Forward

For any organization, remaining up and running no matter what is good business. To do so, develop a risk-intelligent culture within your supply chain business units. While the focus of business continuity planning addresses major interruptions and disasters, it also allows an organization to reduce downtime during routine events. When developing continuity strategies, make sure the process encompasses all links. Consider the supply chain big picture, internal and external; plan for backups for people who carry out critical functions; and understand IT systems and the other technology that supports supply chain operations. Select risk-resistant business partners, continue to monitor the financial status throughout the term of the contract, and provide assistance in business continuity planning to your suppliers.

→ Determine whether the business continuity capabilities of suppliers, contractors, and outsourcing companies are considered in your procurement or selection process.

→ If yes, review the business continuity planning standards that suppliers and other business partners are expected to meet.

→ Determine the time frame for when IT systems that support your department's operations will be restored following a disaster that impacts the data center.

→ Find out whether there are streamlined procurement processes that can be activated if needed.

→ Review your organization's emergency contact procedures with all department employees.

→ Check contact lists of employees, suppliers, contractors, and outsourcing companies to be certain the information is accurate.

→ Ascertain whether cross-training is available to qualify additional employees to carry out time-critical tasks.

CHAPTER *8*

Business Continuity Plan Documents

DEVELOPING A BUSINESS continuity plan is a must in an organization's overall efforts to prepare for, respond to, and continue or restore operations following a disaster. Because of an everchanging environment, constantly evolving technology, unforeseen circumstances, and other variables, a plan will not always be 100 percent successful as originally written. However, if it is comprehensive, well-written, and based on a sound planning process, a plan greatly increases the chance for successful response and recovery.

The Purpose of Business Continuity Plans

There is immeasurable value to be gained from the planning process, and a written plan is needed to capture and document the strategies and procedures developed during that process. The plan provides a general overview of the business continuity program (BCP) and becomes the operating manual when disaster strikes by providing the guidance needed to continue or restore operations. Information and directions detailed in the plan make it possible for the appointed business continuity teams to keep the business operational or to get it back up and running in the shortest time possible. The ultimate result of a continuity program documented in a well-crafted, workable plan may be the difference between the organization surviving and prospering, barely getting by, or even no longer existing following a disaster.

While one purpose of a plan is to codify the BCP, of equal importance is that it provide guidance and direction for carrying out continuity strategies when a disaster occurs. An organization's business continuity plan needs to cover both the proactive and reactive elements of the BCP: proactive—the planning process and ongoing training, testing, and updating; and reactive—the actions to take when disaster strikes. The plan must be specific enough to provide adequate guidance and direction, but also generic enough to allow an effective response to each specific and unique disaster situation that may occur.

The proactive portion of the plan:

→ Sets forth business continuity policy, such as emergency provisions and succession plans.

→ Identifies appropriate confidentiality and proprietary controls for the plan.

→ Defines business continuity standards and requirements applicable throughout the enterprise.

→ Identifies legal, regulatory, and audit requirements.

→ Establishes the organization's business continuity organization and reporting structure.

→ Establishes plan ownership, both of the overall program and of the individual plan components.

→ Documents what is and what is not covered by the plan.

→ Provides guidelines for declaring a disaster and activating the plan—the who, be it an individual or group; the how; and the when—as well as related communications protocols.

→ Assigns responsibility for plan management at each level within the organization.

→ Establishes the process and schedule for testing and training.

→ Formalizes the process and schedule for plan reviews and updates.

The reactive portion of the plan documents strategies and provides the information and direction necessary for those responsible to successfully carry out and maintain the organization's continuity program. It establishes:

→ Business unit continuity team organization, staffing, and reporting structure

→ What needs to be done, listing each business unit's time-critical functions

→ Who is responsible for doing it, including continuity team staffing and assigning responsibility for carrying out continuity procedures

→ How continuity teams will be notified and how plans will be activated

→ Why it needs to be done, addressing internal and external interdependencies

→ When it needs to be done, based on recovery time objectives

→ Where it will be done, including, if there are alternative location arrangements, where to go, who goes, how they get there, and the length of expected or maximum stay

→ How it will be done, including work-around procedures specific to each business unit

→ Resources needed for getting it done, including equipment and data

→ Where resources will come from and how they will be delivered, including primary and backup sources

As previously stated, the people who will implement the plan should be involved in its development. Doing so brings subject-matter knowledge to the process, provides an ongoing reality check, creates buy-in, and ensures that everyone involved is familiar with plan terminology. In addition, since this is a train-as-you-go approach, if the people who will be implementing the plan assist in writing it, the initial training process will be shortened significantly.

Developing the Plan

All the necessary ingredients are in place to put together the business continuity plan—hazards have been identified and mitigated, business functions have been ranked in order of criticality, and strategies have been developed together with an organizational structure to carry out the strategies. You are ready to develop the plan.

It is interesting to consider that this important document is one we hope to never have to use. Yet when it is necessary to do so, an effective plan can be the difference between the loss of your organization and its survival. It is therefore absolutely critical that plans are workable and provide teams with quality guidance.

Start with the basics, perhaps a mock-up of what the plan will look like when it is completed. Have a full understanding of the scope of the plan and where it integrates with other plans. Consider who will be using the plan and how to make it user-friendly. Creating an effective plan is a step-by-step process and not the place for taking shortcuts.

The Basics

Plans need to be both easy to use and easy to maintain. Some very basic guidelines can help accomplish this:

→ For hard-copy plans, use a three-ring binder. When revisions are made, it's easy to replace old pages with the revised versions, avoiding the need to reprint the entire document. It also makes it easy to take pages out to use during a disaster.

→ Avoid concerns about aesthetics. This is a working document. Focus on how it will work, not how it looks.

→ Avoid concerns about whether the plan is long enough. Again, this is a working document. Keep in mind that heft does not equal value. It's the value of the content, not the number of pages that is important. Make the plan long enough to define the program and give sufficient direction to those who will be carrying out the procedures . . . and not one word more.

→ Use an easy-to-read font. Times New Roman in 12-point type is often recommended.

→ Include a detailed table of contents and printed binder divider tabs. This makes it possible to find specific content without having to look through the entire plan.

→ Include a glossary of business continuity terminology and all acronyms. Not everyone using the plan speaks continuity-ese.

→ Use single-sided pages, which makes it easier to update a single page or two and provides space for notes on the opposing blank page.

→ Avoid solid pages of text. Use short paragraphs, bulleted lists, diagrams, and charts for more user-friendly documents.

→ Refer to people by title rather than name to avoid the need to make frequent changes to the body of the plan. List names together with contact information in attachments.

→ Avoid using footnotes.

→ Use clear, plain language.

→ Use attachments for information that is frequently updated (such as lists of names or contact information). Attachments are located at the end of the plan document, making them readily available to use and easy to remove for updates and revisions.

→ Use appendices or annexes for lengthy, detailed information or instructions.

→ Build in a process to track all plan reviews and updates to serve as an audit trail.

→ *Date and number each page of the document* and use revision numbers to help ensure that everyone is using the same version of the plan.

→ If your organization has document standards, take them into account as well when developing the plan.

Plans: Mine, Yours, Ours

An organization's business continuity program is not necessarily documented in a single plan. While one plan may be adequate to cover a small to midsize business, it may not be sufficient to encompass the entire organization of a business that is large or complex in structure. To avoid unwieldy multi-volume documents and to simplify the continuity process, plans and procedures can be broken down into more manageable, functional subplans. If there are multiple divisions, branches, or locations that are widely scattered geographically, each location and division should have its own business continuity team and subplan. In other words, each location has its own subplan and team to which the various departments or business units at that location report.

The business continuity team organization structure must be defined early on. The number of business continuity teams and the size of each team are determined by the number of people needed to carry out the continuity strategies and procedures and the size and configuration of the organization. (Appendix D includes five continuity team models as well as some guidelines for team member and business continuity center location selection.) While the team structure may vary, it is essential that each team have a leader with the authority necessary to make and approve decisions that enable the team to carry out its responsibility. This includes making work schedules and assigning personnel to carry out the schedules, allocating resources, and making expenditures necessary to carry out the strategies outlined in the plan document.

After the company establishes its business continuity organization structure, a coordinated and integrated "family of plans" is created. As shown in Figure 8-1, plans are developed and maintained to provide guidance for each level of the continuity organization structure:

FIGURE 8-1.

BUSINESS CONTINUITY ORGANIZATION AND PLAN STRUCTURE.

→ Corporate business continuity plan

→ Division or location business continuity plans

→ Department/business unit business continuity plans, including IT's disaster recovery plan

Organizations that have employees who regularly work outside the company's facilities, such as service or repair technicians or construction crews, may also include field operations business continuity plans.

It is not necessary that the detailed continuity procedures for all departments be shared throughout the organization. Although there are some differences in content among plans, each department plan needs to include only the information necessary for that business unit to accomplish its continuity responsibilities.

As an example, the continuity plan for a shipping and receiving department includes specific procedures for carrying out the identified time-critical functions following a disaster, whether that disaster results from a loss of IT system support, a contracted shipping company suddenly going out of business, or damage to the building requiring temporary relocation. Among the specific functions likely addressed are:

→ Receiving and processing orders

→ Picking goods for shipment

→ Preparing goods for transit, possibly including hazardous materials

→ Determining the best method of shipment

→ Preparing labels, invoices, packing slips, purchase orders to carriers, and other documents

→ Maintaining an inventory of products, containers, and packing goods

→ Loading and unloading goods

→ Unpacking and routing goods to the warehouse, storage, or internal recipient(s)

→ Following safe storage and handling procedures, including those for any hazardous materials

→ Meeting security and loss prevention requirements

→ Maintaining internal record-keeping systems

→ Tracking shipments

The people responsible for continuity procedures for shipping and receiving require detailed procedures for how to continue or restore these functions. Those at the corporate level do not, nor do other departments such as accounts payable or IT.

One advantage of having individual, stand-alone business unit plans is that in the event of a serious disruption that impacts only a single business unit, the situation can be handled by that business unit using its continuity plan without activating the company's entire continuity organization. If the situation escalates, it is possible to then activate the larger business continuity organization.

While plans can be business unit–specific, they must also include procedures and mechanisms for all the various plans and the teams that carry them out to coordinate and communicate. When carrying out your department's continuity strategies requires coordination or interaction with other departments, work closely with the continuity teams from those business units to ensure that the procedures in both or all plans are synchronized. Do not base your plan on what you think or assume other business units will do.

The Plan Development Process

Developing continuity strategies can be quite a challenge. Creating the plan should be approached as you would any major business document. Think in terms of a step-by-step process with multiple iterations of the plan.

Review requirements and guidelines. In preparing to develop the plan, review company business continuity standards and policies as well as any relevant industry standards, regulations, and audit reports. Also revisit the business impact analysis results, in particular your department's time-critical business functions and recovery time objectives. If a department plan is being developed at the direction of a business continuity manager, he or she will likely be able to provide specific instructions, guidelines, and perhaps a template to use as a guide.

Establish the plan outline by identifying the topics to be covered. Again, if there is a business continuity manager, he or she may be able to provide a working outline that can then be tailored for your business unit.

Assign the development of sections of the plan to each team member. No one individual can develop a comprehensive plan singlehandedly. Involve the entire planning team and, to the extent possible, those who will be implementing the plan. This both shares the workload and brings more subject-matter expertise to the process.

Create a working first draft. Once all individuals have written their assigned sections of the plan, combine the sections, check for and correct inconsistencies in formatting, look for gaps and overlaps, and make any necessary changes and adjustments.

Circulate the working draft to members of the group for review and comment. If a department continuity plan is being developed at the request of the organization's business continuity manager, ask that the manager review the work to date.

Conduct a *tabletop exercise*, which is a verbal walkthrough of actions taken in response to a disaster, using only the plan draft. Have participants keep notes on plan deficiencies and areas needing correction, clarification, or a greater level of detail. During the exercise, consider if carrying out the procedures in the plan will result in meeting RTOs.

Incorporate identified improvements in a second draft. Revise, clarify, and enhance the plan based on comments from team members and what was learned in the tabletop exercise.

Repeat the process used for draft one. Circulate the second draft to group members for review and comment. Again, ask for a review by the business continuity manager or other individual who is responsible for the organization's business continuity program. Then, conduct a second tabletop exercise.

At this point in the plan development process, consider some reality checks:

→ If your organization has bargaining units, be certain that what is being asked of employees does not conflict with union contracts and possibly create a secondary disaster.

→ Check to make sure that the plan is not overdocumented. Remember, not a word more than is necessary. Documents that are too wordy or too lengthy can create confusion and lead to time wasted in trying to find needed information. If your organization has technical writers, consider whether it might be helpful to have them review the plan and offer some suggestions for improvement.

→ As appropriate, have the plan reviewed and approved by upper management, auditors, the individual or department responsible for regulatory compliance, and other interested parties and groups to avoid having to make changes once the first full edition of the plan is complete.

→ Get an additional review and approval from the organization's legal counsel. This may result in the addition of a disclaimer in the front section of the document that includes a brief statement of the purpose of the document and a caveat that while the plan is regularly tested, revised, and updated, some elements of the plan such as RTOs can be affected by unforeseen circumstances when an actual disaster occurs.

→ Write the plan as though on the day the initial plan is finalized, every person involved in the writing process will walk out the door and never return. Check the plan to ensure that there is sufficient guidance so it can be carried out even if the people who wrote it are not available to explain or expand on any part of the document.

Based on the results of the tabletop exercise and feedback from all who have reviewed the document, make any necessary changes. Then, once again, have all team members review the document and agree that it is ready for distribution. While two drafts may be sufficient, do not be taken aback if an additional draft or drafts are necessary. Creating a first version of a plan takes time, particularly when team members have little or no business continuity experience or have limited time available to devote to the project.

Avoid using the word "final" in referring to a plan document. A plan is never "done" but is always a work in progress. What you have at this point is a completed first version of the plan.

Print and distribute the document. It is not necessary that every employee of the company or the business unit have a copy of the full plan. Consider numbering all printed copies of the plan to control distribution and ensure that all plan holders receive all revisions and updates. If possible, conduct a meeting with those receiving copies of the document to go through the plan with them. Otherwise, include a cover letter reminding plan recipients of its history and purpose.

Maintain current copies of all plan documents off-site in the event a disaster prevents access to your buildings or computer systems are not operational. Consider making sure that each member of the business continuity teams can access their business continuity plan from any computer with an Internet connection as well as their mobile devices with appropriate password and other security protection.

Finally, congratulate yourself and the team members on a job well done.

Support Tools

In addition to receiving the actual plan, continuity team members need tools that make their jobs easier. Think in technology product terms. When you buy a new cell phone or printer for your home computer, there's the big manual and the quick reference guide or basic steps in a one-page format. Along with the plan document itself (the big manual), each team member should be provided with some form of quick start guide. The information contained in this quick start guide is taken directly from plan documents and supports fast and accurate actions and decision making by the continuity teams, particularly in the first hours while everyone is getting organized and into continuity mode. A guide can include the criteria and process for activating the business continuity plan and the team, initial notifications to be made, and initial steps upon arrival at the assigned location.

A five-inch by seven-inch guide produced as a flip chart is one option for providing this information. Such a chart is inexpensive to produce. Each team member can have three copies: one for the office, one for home, and one for the briefcase or car. A pocket on the inside back cover can be included to hold a list of emergency contact numbers.

Provide each team member with an individualized check-

FIGURE 8-2.

SAMPLE DEPARTMENT BUSINESS CONTINUITY TEAM ACTIVATION CHECKLIST.

☐ Report to the department's business continuity center in accordance with the activation schedule or as directed.

☐ Check in at the security desk; display your photo identification and sign the check-in list.

☐ Report to the assigned work location and check in with the department business continuity team manager.

☐ Gather your copy of the business continuity plan and business continuity supplies and equipment.

☐ Review printed emergency procedures and building evacuation routes.

☐ Call the disaster recovery team at the number provided to establish your temporary log-in information and receive your temporary password.

☐ Determine if your assigned computer has access to the software and files you require; call the disaster recovery team for assistance, if necessary.

☐ Follow the assigned procedures outlined in the department business continuity plan.

☐ Initiate and maintain a written time record and log.

☐ Attend the initial team briefing conducted by the team manager.

list with actual tick boxes that outlines the initial steps they are to take when disaster strikes (see Figure 8-2). A five-inch by seven-inch laminated card format works well for this checklist.

The reverse side of the card can list emergency contact numbers and possibly directions to the pre-identified alternate work location.

You can provide easy-to-access information on laminated wallet cards or stickers that can be placed on the back of building access badges. Include business continuity contact information and initial plan activation steps. This same information can be produced in magnet form for team members to keep on their home refrigerator. Another alternative is electronic versions of this information, made available for team members to download onto mobile applications.

Organizations might also consider creating a Web portal to make alerts, disaster notifications, activation instructions, and information updates available to employees wherever they may be located.

Just as with the plan document itself, all of these tools—hard copy or electronic—must be updated with every plan revision, and as with plan documents, they should be dated. Incorrect or outdated information is dangerous no matter how it is delivered.

Avoiding Plan Gaps

When reviewing plans, I find that three important areas are often overlooked: damage assessment, communication, and deactivation.

Damage Assessment

A damage assessment is a critical function that must be performed as soon as conditions allow following any significant disruption or disaster. If there is no damage to the physical plant, the assessment focuses on the status of operations, such as whether shipments are being sent and received, employees are on hand to carry out time-critical functions, and computer systems support is available. If there is physical damage, the assessment provides an accurate picture both of the amount of physical damage done and the impact of the disaster on business operations. This in turn determines the level of business continuity team activation required and provides information needed to begin long-term planning for full restoration of operations.

Responsibility for conducting assessments is preassigned in the continuity plan, and detailed checklists for conducting each of the assessments are provided. In larger organizations, there can be a damage assessment team, perhaps headed by a member of the facilities and engineering staff. In many cases, a representative of one of the business units who is familiar with the department's equipment and operational requirements is assigned to the assessment team. To avoid any possible risk to employees, if the disaster results in physical damage to facilities, assessments are conducted only when the building is safe, entry has been approved by public officials, and there is no threat to the safety and well-being of those conducting the assessment.

As a rule, three types of assessments are conducted:

1. An *initial general assessment*, conducted by walking through the site. The overall status of structures and contents is noted: what has been destroyed, what incurred major damage, what incurred minor damage, or what is unaffected. The initial assessment also includes verifying the availability of electrical power, telecommunications systems, water service, and computer systems. An external check is performed to determine whether there is access to structures and the site.

2. A *detailed damage assessment*, which provides a full and complete report of the status of facilities, infrastructure, office furnishings, equipment, supplies, inventory, and technical support systems. This assessment provides a more complete picture of exactly what has been damaged and whether it can be salvaged or restored or must be replaced, and the full impact of the event on operations. This assessment can also provide an initial estimate of the length of time required to restore operations. (Some organizations also opt to include an initial estimate of what losses may be covered by insurance.) This information, together with the nature of the disaster and the prognosis for reentering damaged buildings, is used to more accurately evaluate the situation and to determine specific strategies for restoring normal operations.

3. *Additional assessments*, which are conducted throughout the activation period either on a preestablished regular basis or as requested by the corporate business continuity team. Together with status reports received from business unit continuity teams, these ongoing assessments provide valuable information about progress being made and any issues that have arisen that will delay restoring full operations.

In some cases and with the prior approval of insurance carriers, damage can be documented using date- and time-stamped video or still-photo media so that cleanup, repair, and initial restoration procedures can be initiated more quickly.

Communication

While disaster communications issues were discussed in Chapter 7, it is important to document the continuity communications requirements and detailed procedures in the plan document. The plan must cover the who, the how, and the when of communicating with the corporate business continuity team, other business unit continuity teams, and employees in addition to customers, suppliers, other critical business partners, and stakeholders.

This critically important communication starts with having a process and assigned responsibility for all initial notifications and updates. Make certain that the plan identifies and details all the people, organizations, and other entities you need to contact immediately upon activation of the plan, throughout the business continuity process, and through full deactivation.

Communication also requires the means to receive and relay messages and information. The department that manages the organization's telecommunications likely has communications mitigation strategies built into its department business continuity plan, such as fail-over phone switches, phone lines from multiple carriers, and phone lines entering the building at different locations. Some organizations opt to use nongeographic phone numbers that divert calls made to the company's existing number to an alternate landline or cellular location in a disaster situation. Landline phones, cellular phones, satellite phones, voice over IP, and e-mail are just some of the options for communications redundancies.

External communications must be considered as well. You do not want customers and clients to think the worst if they have heard that your organization experienced a major emergency or disaster and they have not heard directly from a representative of your organization in a timely manner. You do not want these customers and clients to consider looking for another source for the service or product you provide. One approach for organizations with call centers is to use the call center and call center representatives as a business continuity contact center, with documented plans and procedures for doing so included in the business continuity plan. An alternative is available from some telecommunications providers that field calls made to your company at a virtual call center facility staffed by their employees. Calls are answered using your organization's name, and messages are taken and then forwarded in accordance with your instructions. While calls not being answered by a company employee is not the ideal situation, even worse is a customer's call going unanswered or a supplier or other business partner hearing a recorded message that your phone number is out of service.

Each department's plan needs to include directions for when and how to use these alternate communications methods.

Deactivation

Another important process to detail in the plan is the deactivation phase—how to return to normal operations once the disaster has passed. This is referred to by IT folks as "failing back." Deactivation is accomplished in logical steps that require attention to details such as switching phone lines, recalling employees, restoring or rerouting deliveries and shipments, ensuring that all files are backed up, returning supplies and equipment, completing and submitting all documentation, and participating in debriefings. Omitting detailed deactivation procedures from a plan can result in a secondary disaster that can be more destructive than the original event.

Reviews and Updates

Plan documents—an essential component of your BCP—are not static and are never complete, never finished. Plans are a perpetual work in progress and, like people and fine wine, they should grow, mature, and get better with time and experience.

The value of even the very best business continuity plan deteriorates quickly if the plan does not keep pace with changes in the organization. A great plan today, left sitting on a shelf for six months or more, likely begins to become out-of-date. Think back over the last year and list the changes that have taken place in your organization as a whole and in the supply chain business units particularly. This short exercise likely indicates the importance of regular plan updates.

Best practices call for conducting a full review or formal audit of the entire plan not less than annually. Interim revisions may be necessary as well as a result of substantive changes in any information contained in the plan, including lessons learned from tests and exercises. The BCP must be revisited regularly to determine whether changes or enhancements in the plan are necessary. On an annual basis, the hazard assessment and business impact analysis also must be reviewed to determine whether changes in strategies and plans are needed. Perhaps the organization's priorities have changed or there are new locations, new product lines, or new processes. Any of these or other operational changes can create a need for plan revisions at one or multiple levels.

Just some of the triggers that signal a need to review and update plans are changes in:

→ Business continuity staffing
→ Suppliers, contractors, and/or outsourcing companies
→ Contact information
→ Operational procedures
→ Technology
→ Physical plant
→ Equipment
→ Hazard information
→ Company policy
→ Regulatory requirements
→ Audit requirements—internal or external

→ Technology such as manufacturing, IT, or telecommunications

→ The organization's size, either growth or downsizing

One of the greatest challenges in maintaining current information in plan documents is the ongoing changes in contact information for employees, customers, critical suppliers, and contractors. A wrong contact name or telephone number can have a negative impact on the amount of time required to restore operations. Partner with your human resources department to keep employee contact information current, and with accounts payable or procurement to maintain current names and contact information for suppliers and other business partners. One way to help ensure that the plan has up-to-date information for external contacts is to periodically give a copy of the plan's contact attachments to an employee and have him or her place calls to the numbers listed to verify that the information on the list is accurate and current.

To help manage the impact that ongoing organizational changes make in business continuity programs, establish documented policies supported by management that require all changes that impact continuity be reported to the person who manages the BCP. If the organization has a change management department or function, link business continuity to the established change management process.

The Effect of Mergers and Other Reorganizations

In today's business environment, mergers, acquisitions, takeovers, and divestitures are the norm, as are major reorganizations. These are all significant changes and as such require a thorough review of hazards, business impacts, strategies, procedures, and plan documents.

There are challenges in maintaining an effective, integrated continuity program following any merger, acquisition, or other far-reaching organizational change. A fact at times not fully considered is that when two or more organizations merge, whatever the reason, the result is a new organization. The new organization is likely larger, has more geographical locations, and offers a wider range of products and services. In addition, it is unlikely that the merging entities have the same suppliers, outsourcing companies, and other business partners.

From a supply chain perspective, this new organization must continue to meet customer needs and requirements within a new organizational structure. The good news is that with the new, larger company, there are likely more business continuity strategy options. The question, however, is whether we use *your* business continuity plan or *my* business continuity plan. Reaching consensus on how to proceed is particularly difficult when both organizations bring mature continuity programs based on sound planning practices to the table. The answer is that we must create *our* plan, a *new plan* that will best meet the continuity needs of the *new organization*.

And while it may be possible to incorporate the best elements of both plans into a new improved plan, in some situations it may be necessary to begin anew. Combining existing plans may not result in a continuity program that meets the needs of the newly formed organization when a merger results in a completely different organizational structure; a significant number of new departments, divisions, or locations; the total reprioritization of core processes; or in the event the merger involves two or more extremely diverse cultures. A collaborative effort in developing a new program may be necessary.

Many of the same issues and challenges must be addressed when individual business units have unilaterally developed business continuity plans that must then be incorporated into a cohesive enterprise-wide continuity program.

Here are just some of the supply chain business continuity issues you may need to deal with when creating a new business continuity organization:

→ Combining differently configured supply chains
→ Integrating people and teams from different supply chain organizations

→ Identifying and addressing additional supply chain risks

→ Working with supply chain systems such as Materials Requirements Planning or other IT support systems that are not fully compatible

→ Working with communications systems that are not fully compatible

→ Meeting additional regulatory or legal requirements

→ Working with organizational cultures that may vary greatly

Conversely, combining two or more organizations can present opportunities, such as:

→ Creating additional continuity strategies as a result of having more locations, operational redundancies, and skilled personnel

→ Combining the best elements of two programs into a new program that results in a greater overall capability

→ Creating continuity teams whose combined members contribute a wider range of experience, capabilities, and know-how

Full advantage can be taken of these opportunities and others by addressing business continuity planning issues during the initial planning stages of a merger or acquisition. This can include:

→ Determining how the business continuity programs will operate while the merger or acquisition process is taking place

→ Identifying and planning for new risks that may arise during the merger process, a time that is definitely not business as usual

→ Addressing the restructuring of the business continuity planning group and forming one group that equitably represents both or all the organizations

→ Establishing a process to review all supply chain contracts to determine if there are overlapping contracts and whether some contracts need to be renegotiated, terminated, or allowed to expire as a result of the merger

→ Conducting a thorough review and audit of both existing BCPs to determine whether the most advantageous path is to combine the best elements of both or all existing programs or to develop a new, fully integrated program that meets the business continuity needs of the newly created organization

Whatever the reason for the revision or update, ensure that all plan holders receive all updates and revisions. If the changes are substantial, provide training for all those with continuity roles to familiarize them with the new plan and their new roles and responsibilities. Check to be certain that all electronic and hard copies of the plan and the related tools and guides are updated.

True story: It was summer during my initial on-site visit with a new client on the East Coast when I sat down to talk with a person who had been a member of a disbanded planning group that had been assigned to write the company's original business continuity plan. When I asked to see a copy of the plan document, the individual pointed to an open office window and said, "Sure, it's right over there." Lo and behold, there was the plan binder propping open an office window. The path from business continuity document to window prop was determined by several factors:

→ While it was titled "business continuity plan," the plan focused only on IT with no consideration of the business of the entire business.

→ Few people outside the original planning group even knew the plan existed.

→ The plan had never been tested.

→ People identified as members of the business continuity team had not been notified that they were members, let alone received any training.

→ The plan was three years old and had never been reviewed or updated, nor was there any mechanism for doing so.

→ Once the plan document was written, the planning group was disbanded and no one was assigned permanent ownership of the plan.

→ The project had as its goal a business continuity *plan* rather than a business continuity *program*.

A Sample Basic Plan

While I am always somewhat hesitant to provide a sample continuity plan, I understand the desire to see an example of what a plan looks like, what information it contains, and how it is formatted. Appendix E contains three sample documents:

1. Table of contents for a corporate business continuity plan
2. Table of contents for a department or other business unit plan
3. Basic plan for a department or other business unit

As the sample plan is generic, it will not necessarily work as a model for every supply chain business unit to develop its plan document. Use the table of contents to develop an outline. Always focus on what your business unit needs to continue or resume operations. Include sufficient direction and guidance to enable team members to carry out their continuity responsibilities. Keep in mind your organization's overall continuity requirements and ensure that your plan integrates and coordinates with all other plans.

A great deal of specific relevant information in the document is contained in its attachments. There, updates can be incorporated into the plan without having to reproduce the entire document. Attachments might be made up of contact lists, resource lists, sample forms, continuity organization charts, detailed procedures needed to carry out your business unit's continuity strategies, instructions for setting up operations at alternate work sites, and an action checklist for each team member.

If you wish to do additional research on developing plans, sources for guidance include the Internet, insurance carriers, purchased plan development software, books, classes, and consultants.

There are quite a number of plan documents available on the Internet, including some that are identified as business continuity plans though in reality they are disaster recovery plans. A great majority of the plans available online are for government agencies, educational institutions, and not-for-profit organizations. Not surprisingly, it is rare that a company publicly shares its continuity plan, as the plan may contain proprietary information or the company may not wish to provide its competition with information about its plan. In addition, companies have invested significant resources in developing their plan and see no value in making the finished products available to others.

Your insurance carrier or broker can often provide guidance with some portions of the planning process, including plan development. There are also software packages on the market that can assist with creating plans. As with all software, be sure to check into all the pluses and minuses and conduct a thorough selection process if you opt to go that route. Avoid a fill-in-the-blanks product.

Helpful information is also available from the Federal Emergency Management Agency (FEMA) and the Department of Homeland Security websites.

Going Forward

For any organization, remaining up and running no matter what the challenges is good business. The business continuity plan is an essential part of a business continuity program. It is where continuity team members turn if there is a disaster or serious interruption.

A good plan that successfully guides the team through a crisis situation can be the difference between success and failure in continuing or restoring time-critical business functions. It is therefore absolutely critical that the plan is workable and that it provides information of sufficient quality and detail to guide the continuity team through the disaster.

→ If your organization or your department has a business continuity plan, review the sections of the plan that cover your job function to determine if it provides the information and guidance needed for you or an alternate to successfully carry out your role in the business unit's continuity procedures. If not, take action to make the necessary updates and improvements.

→ Check your copy of the business continuity plan to be certain that it contains the most current versions of the basic plan and all appendices and attachments.

→ Using the sections of this chapter on "Developing the Plan" and "The Basics," review your existing plan to identify possible areas for improvement.

→ Review plan attachments to determine if contact information needed by your department is included and current.

→ Meet with a representative of the telecommunications business unit to gain an understanding of the company's disaster communications capabilities and strategies, and include detailed directions for using redundant or alternate communications methods in your business unit's continuity plan.

→ If there is no plan for supply chain departments, meet with supply chain managers to outline the contents of a plan.

→ Determine if there are tools to support the plan such as checklists and guides.

→ If there are no tools or aids, consider developing some basic guides for your department, perhaps starting with a list of emergency contact information in a format such as a laminated wallet card.

CHAPTER 9

Testing and Maintaining Business Continuity Plans

OLLOWING THE DEVELOPMENT of plan documents, the next step in the business continuity planning lifecycle is to test and implement plans while continuing the on-going process of maintaining the program and incorporating business continuity into the day-to-day operations and culture of the organization.

A program of training, exercises, and tests, providing all employees with the appropriate level of education and training, is an integral part of any business continuity program that moves plans beyond the concept stage. A continuity awareness and training program for all employees underpins any organization's capability to manage disasters and helps ensure that all employees understand what the organization is prepared to do and are aware of the part they must play.

A plan is not a plan until it has been tested; it is only theory, paper in a binder. Exercises and tests provide the best possible reality check for your plans other than an actual disaster.

To ensure that the plan is workable, doable, and provides the necessary guidance, personnel must be trained and the plan's strategies must be tested. Staff assigned to business continuity teams need tailored, detailed training that focuses on their particular roles. This can be accomplished through tabletop and simulation exercises and specialized live (field) tests. Think of exercises and tests as disaster rehearsals, an opportunity to learn critically important lessons before an actual disaster occurs. It is through ongoing tests and exercises that we work out the kinks, enhance strategies, and help ensure a successful return to normal business operations.

By its very nature, the supply chain in every organization is changing and adapting almost continually to meet the demands of today's fast-paced global business environment. It is essential to regularly test, review, and revise the program and plan documents to maintain the capability to successfully respond to the dynamic and ever changing nature of risk and the requirements of conducting business today.

Training, Exercises, and Tests: The Key to Workable Plans

The business continuity plan should assign responsibility for maintaining a comprehensive training program and outline the requisite goals and objectives for the program. Good teamwork must involve those who manage business continuity and other related programs, such as disaster recovery and emergency preparedness and response, as well as representatives from human resources and security. Such teamwork helps make certain that the necessary training is delivered without gaps, redundancies, or overlaps and reinforces working relationships among the business units. When practical, continuity training should be combined with disaster recovery, emergency response, safety, and security training.

In the event the organization does not have a formal training and testing program, an individual business unit can unilaterally conduct training and exercises. While this is not as efficient as an enterprise-wide program, such limited training is a must in preparing the department and its employees to respond when disasters occur.

A big-picture approach can be used to develop an annual

program of orientation sessions, drills, training, exercises, and tests that fulfills the requirements outlined in the plan. This all-inclusive method of long-range planning and scheduling gets these training opportunities on everyone's calendar well ahead of scheduled dates, which helps to ensure the availability of people and training facilities. A curriculum outline should be developed for each training component. The outline should include to whom the training is directed, how often it is to be conducted and by whom, content overview, and the length of time required for the training.

Once there is adequate knowledge of the organization's existing policies, plans, and procedures and a basic understanding of the overall approach to addressing disasters and threats, a more complete picture of the organization's programs begins to emerge.

Remember to include primary and all alternate team members in training sessions and exercises. And once your plan is mature, consider including suppliers, contractors, and even customers in exercises. Doing so increases the realism, expands learning, and provides opportunities for partnering in business continuity planning.

Training

Employees are an organization's greatest asset, and every individual makes a contribution to the organization every day and will continue doing so in the wake of a disaster. *All* employees, from the mail room to the executive offices, are critical to the success of first-rate business continuity and related programs, and all need to receive the appropriate level of business continuity education and training. For most, this entails the basics—what programs exist, the purpose of each, what it means for the employees, what they can expect from the organization when disaster strikes, and what the organization expects of them.

All employees are responsible for following business continuity policies and procedures, yet it is often the employees not assigned to continuity teams who fall between the cracks and do not receive sufficient training. Remember that for each of us, our perception is our reality. The perception of employees who are not aware of programs and plans for managing disasters is that the programs and plans do not exist, and for them, that is the reality.

Establish a comprehensive program that includes the necessary level of training for all employees. Start with orientation and basic training in continuity. For newly hired employees, this should begin with their orientation; for older employees, it can start at their annual review. Every employee should be made aware of the mutual expectations—what they are to do, what the organization will do, and how the organization's disaster communications procedures work. In the case of a business continuity program, it is possible that when a disaster happens, some employees are simply to wait to receive instructions for when and where to report. While this sounds simple, employees who do not know this is the case can create confusion and extra unnecessary work when a disaster strikes.

Orientation and refresher training should include a review of the organization's disaster-related policies. For example, if there is a policy that employees are not to make statements to the media, be sure they know that is the case and provide them with the name and contact information of the person to whom media representatives are to be referred. Also, periodically survey employees to determine their level of awareness and in what areas they need further training.

Training can be classroom, computer-based, or exercise-based. Articles in organization newsletters and on the intranet and announcements at department and other work group meetings can help reinforce the training and provide an avenue to update employees on simple revisions to plans and procedures.

Awareness and training programs are critical for embedding business continuity management into the culture of the organization. As a further step in making continuity part of core business practices, some organizations are tying participation in continuity training and exercises to annual performance reviews and compensation.

For those with specific business continuity responsibilities, training provides an opportunity to develop practical knowledge of the plan and its procedures. Continuity team members also gain a more complete understanding of their roles: what to do, why it is being done, and where it fits in the bigger continuity picture.

For assigned team members, training must go well beyond handing someone a plan document or checklist of actions and assuming there is complete understanding of the assigned duties. Individuals involved in carrying out plans must not only understand what to do. They should also have a firm understanding of the importance of their role. Tailored, detailed training that focuses on team members' specific roles results in an in-depth understanding of how the actions each team member takes fit in the overall picture. This level of understanding has been shown to be the largest factor contributing to employee compliance with established policies and preparedness activities prior to an event and to following continuity procedures following a disaster.

Training should result in every employee in every department possessing an understanding of the organization's approach to business continuity management and how his or her department is integrated in the total program. Training should also result in all employees knowing what they would need to do to continue critical operations and where the equipment, supplies, and people needed to get it done are located.

Exercises and Tests

There are only two reasons for conducting exercises and tests: We need to *test* plans, and we need to *train* people. (While "exercise" is the preferred business continuity terminology, "test" is more commonly used in disaster recovery.)

Beyond basic business continuity orientation and detailed training, exercises and tests provide continuity team members with advanced training. They also offer an opportunity to identify needed improvements to strategies and plans before a disaster occurs. Team building is an additional benefit for continuity team members who do not work together on a regular basis.

Begin by determining the purpose and objectives for the exercise. Choose the best exercise type for the situation and the maturity of the company's business continuity programs and teams. There are three basic and increasingly challenging exercise categories: tabletop, simulation, and live.

A *tabletop exercise* (also called a walkthrough or desktop exercise) is nonstressful and slow-paced. It is used to evaluate strategies, plans, and procedures and to provide a training opportunity for team members. In a tabletop exercise, a facilitator presents and continues to develop a disaster scenario. Team members discuss the situation and problem-solve using the plan document, in the process becoming more familiar with their roles. The length of a tabletop exercise is typically two to four hours, including the debriefing process.

A *simulation exercise* (also called a functional exercise) is designed to give team members a more realistic, hands-on experience in dealing with a disaster situation. It is faster paced and more stressful than a tabletop exercise. It enhances communications and decision-making skills and helps further familiarize team members with the plan, its procedures, and their roles.

A simulation exercise involves two groups. One is the business continuity team; the other is a simulation team. Prior to the exercise, the simulation team—working with an agreed-upon, realistic disaster scenario and scope—develops messages that in the event of a real disaster might be received by the continuity team from anyone, anywhere, inside or outside the organization. This can include employees, customers, suppliers, outsourcing companies, regulatory agencies, stockholders, government agencies, media representatives, and public safety officials. Once the exercise starts, the simulation team begins sending the predeveloped messages to the business continuity team—in writing, by phone, electronically, or in person. The continuity team members must then decide what actions are needed to respond to the messages received. To continue to advance the disaster scenario, the simulation team continues to draft and send new messages based on the actions taken by the continuity team. To be fully effective, test actions must mirror reality. All actions taken by continuity team members must be based on existing plans and procedures and resources that actually exist. Plan on a minimum of half a day for a simulation exercise, though some last for a full business day from opening briefing through the debriefing process.

A simulation exercise provides an excellent opportunity to provide training for primary and backup continuity team members. Start by having the backups serve as members of the simulation team while the primary members participate in the exercise. In subsequent exercises, reverse the roles. You can also combine primary and backup members on both the exercise team and the simulation team. Simulation team members often report that being a member of the simulation team is as valuable a learning experience as is participating in the exercise as a continuity team member.

A *live exercise* (also called a field or full-scale exercise) is based on a disaster scenario and involves the actual mobilization of business continuity teams and resources. It can be limited to selected parts of an organization or encompass the entire enterprise. This type of exercise adds further integration and coordination components to the simulation. Just as in an actual disaster, the scenario may include inaccessible buildings; the necessity to relocate people and resources, perhaps to an alternate work site; and computer systems being down while the disaster recovery team restores IT operations at an internal or contracted *hot site*. (A hot site is a remote, alternate, backup computer operations location equipped with compatible hardware and the infrastructure needed to support IT operations.) Live exercises can include actual continuity procedures such as redirecting shipments, activating manual work-around procedures, and functions being fulfilled by cross-trained backup employees. The most realistic of all exercises, a live exercise takes more time and resources to plan and conduct. Exercises can be conducted during regular business hours, though it is not uncommon for live exercises to be held at night or on the weekend. Some extend for two or more days.

When a disaster recovery test—a live exercise conducted by the disaster recovery team—includes testing restoration of supply chain IT support systems, the test provides an excellent opportunity to coordinate with the disaster recovery team. Supply chain business units can assist by determining the level of success in recovering servers and applications related to a wide range of functions, such as receiving advanced shipment notifications, orders, and buyer approvals; generating pick and pack manifests; or tracking shipments. The cooperative effort provides the disaster recovery team with a more realistic test environment and offers the participating supply chain functions an opportunity to exercise their business continuity plans.

Exercise Scenario Selection

In general, exercises raise awareness and provide a team-building opportunity, as well as identifying needed corrections, improvements, and enhancements to plans and strategies. New lessons are learned with every exercise and test, as well as when disasters occur. To be certain that plans incorporate the lessons learned by those who have been impacted by recent actual major disasters, include a broad range of scenarios that incorporate realistic challenges:

→ A critical supplier of components for multiple manufacturing plants or a niche supplier of a critical specialty part suddenly goes out of business.

→ An explosion causes significant damage to an outsourced warehouse facility and its contents.

→ A computer virus infects the e-mail system, requiring a total shutdown of the system for at least thirty-six hours while the situation is corrected and additional safeguards are installed.

→ Attempts to notify key employees who are expected to carry out business continuity responsibilities are unsuccessful.

→ Air transportation in a 250-mile radius of the company's location is shut down for three days.

→ A long-term electrical power outage is caused by severe winter storms and there is a resulting shortage of fuel for generators.

→ Employees of your primary contracted transport company call a strike and walk off the job.

→ As a result of a workplace violence incident resulting in life-threatening injuries, the police department has declared the building a crime scene and it has been evacuated. It is not known when the investigation will be completed and access to the building allowed.

Make sure the scenario selected is realistic and has a high probability of occurring. Limit the use of *worst-case scenarios*—the maximum intensity of a specific hazard, coupled with the maximum estimated impact on operations—particularly when testing new plans or training newly named continuity teams. When exercising new teams, a worst-case scenario may be too overwhelming and the resulting high levels of stress can prevent learning. An accompanying outcome can be a failure to identify needed plan improvements. Start with the simple and build to the more complex with a series of increasingly challenging and stressful scenarios.

After teams have exercised with less demanding scenarios such as a power outage, an IT failure, or loss of a supplier, use a likely worst-case scenario that would have the greatest impact on operations, such as loss of a facility due to fire or widespread natural disaster, to fully test plans and provide advanced training.

Once people are comfortable with their roles and responsibilities and plans are more mature, continue to vary the severity and type of event presented in the scenario to ensure covering a wide range of possible disasters that require scaling the response appropriately to match the scenario.

Department and business unit tests and exercises can be conducted separately, with IT in a disaster recovery test, or as part of overarching, organization-wide exercises and tests. Department continuity teams use their plan and any materials documented in their plan that would reasonably be available within the scenario. Some scenarios eliminate resources (such as phone or data communications, a facility, or a sole source supplier), while others remove team members or other key players from the exercise.

Once the business continuity program is in place and a series of exercises and tests have been conducted, consider the value and advisability of including customers, suppliers, or other business partners in the testing process. As an example, if your organization's plan includes shipping to a customer from a more distant secondary location when the primary location experiences a disaster, ask the customer to participate in a test or exercise. Determine whether the redirecting strategies meet your customer's requirements or would result in a need for the customer to activate some of its continuity procedures, such as increasing shipments from an alternate supplier. This provides you with an opportunity to test continuity strategies and plans and to partner with your customer in developing improved strategies when necessary.

Capturing the Lessons Learned

While exercises have enormous importance as a training vehicle, the greatest value comes when the lessons to be learned are fully captured and acted upon. During the exercise, have observers note team members' level of ease in using their plans, executing their tasks, communicating with fellow team members, and meeting the challenges of the scenario. Exercise participants should maintain a log and take notes on issues and challenges that arise during the exercise.

Conduct a debriefing session as soon as possible following the exercise to identify what worked well, what did not work as planned, and what needs to be done to improve strategies, procedures, and the plan document. I prefer to use both a group discussion and a written exercise evaluation form for debriefing. Determine the level of effectiveness of the plan documents and whether team members need additional training and more frequent exercises. Capture and document the lessons learned, outline what needs to happen to resolve problems, and assign responsibility for completion of each identified corrective action item with a specific deliverable date for each assignment. Begin preparations for your next exercise.

The success of an exercise or test can be measured by the level of achievement in reaching the exercise goals and objectives as well as by whether or not the exercise resulted in meeting the established recovery time objectives. The purpose of an exercise is not to reach perfection but to *test* plans, *train* people, and identify ways to improve. If there were no issues or challenges and the teams performed perfectly, it is likely that the scenario was not sufficiently challenging.

Plan Reviews and Maintenance

The task of looking for gaps and areas needing improvement in the organization's business continuity plans should continue throughout the training and testing processes. Based on observations during an exercise and feedback obtained in the debriefing, needed plan enhancements and improvements may include:

→ Providing greater detail in identified sections of the plan

→ Revising notification and activation procedures that did not work as planned

→ Changing the continuity team structure or adding additional team positions

→ Adding more communications equipment in the business continuity center

→ Inserting detailed procedures for improved customer interfaces

→ Improving strategies for meeting all service level agreements

→ Assigning responsibility for meeting applicable regulatory requirements

→ Providing more details about alternate work locations, such as maps and directions for how to get there and security clearance procedures

➔ Reviewing more frequently all attachments listing contact information for all internal and external key contacts

➔ Enacting better controls to track distribution of the plan to make certain all team members receive all plan revisions and updates

Going Forward

Experience almost always identifies needed changes in plans. The hope is that the experience will be a test or exercise rather than an actual disaster.

A program of training and testing that includes all employees can help ensure that all individuals are aware of the part they play and understand what the organization is prepared to do. Exercises and tests provide the best possible reality check for your plans other than a disaster and are a training opportunity for continuity team members and others who have a role in carrying out continuity plans. Plans must be reviewed and updated frequently to ensure that the information they contain is accurate and current. The overall result is a better prepared organization capable of continuing time-critical operations when future disasters occur.

➔ Poll the people in your business unit to determine whether they have received sufficient business continuity training.

➔ Work with supply chain business unit managers to develop and schedule regular continuity program refresher briefings for all employees.

➔ Develop a scenario and conduct a tabletop exercise for your business unit's continuity team.

➔ Meet with representatives of other supply chain business units to explore conducting joint training and exercises.

➔ Volunteer to be a member of the simulation team for the next planned simulation exercise.

➔ Ask to be included in the next disaster recovery test of your department's IT support systems.

CHAPTER 10

Business Continuity Standards, Regulations, and Requirements

A S BUSINESS CONTINUITY planning further matures, the search continues for improvements and methods to measure levels of continuity competency. Any inclusive discussion of business continuity today requires addressing the rapidly changing regulations, guidelines, and standards that directly and indirectly impact how the sufficiency of a continuity program is measured.

Specific guidance is invaluable when a new continuity program is being developed and in the continuing efforts to identify ways to improve an existing program. There is a need to know that steps being taken will result in the organization being better prepared and more capable and that stakeholders can be assured that current best practices are used to maintain an acceptable level of continuity competency.

There is an accompanying business need by organizations for an objective method to assess the continuity capability of suppliers, outsourcing companies, and other groups that support time-critical functions that are essential to the core operations of the organization. Equally important is that organizations have a way of determining that the companies and individuals with whom they contract for continuity services and planning assistance are qualified.

Regulations, Planning Guidelines, and Standards

With enterprise risk management increasingly seen as a core business practice, there has been an upsurge of interest and new developments around continuity regulations, guidelines, and standards. After almost twenty-five years of slowly increasing activity, the events of 9/11 and the increasing interest in and need for business continuity standards has resulted in a significant increase in the volume and frequency of actions in these areas.

Regulations

Some organizations must follow regulations, created and enforced by recognized regulatory bodies, that include business continuity requirements. Regulations require compliance, and failure to meet them can result in fines, penalties, or sanctions. At the federal level in the United States, some of the agencies that have regulations are the Government Accountability Office (GAO), Securities and Exchange Commission (SEC), Federal Reserve, Federal Electric Reliability Council (FERC), North American Electric Reliability Council (NERC), Joint Commission on Accreditation of Healthcare Organizations (JCAHO), and the Food and Drug Administration (FDA). Typically, the regulations are very specific in nature and are usually mandated and punitive. They require organizations to develop and maintain continuity capability. Many state and local authorities have the same requirements. Recently, a partial list of U.S. regulations that included business continuity implications numbered over 120, and it is highly unlikely that the list will ever stop growing—at least as long as there are lawmakers and public officials. New regulations and laws will almost certainly be frequently added to the list.

For companies with global operations, the requirements in the country where they are based may be only the tip of the iceberg. Every country in which they conduct business may have its own set of regulations that must also be followed.

Planning Guidelines

Guidelines are produced by professional organizations and set best practices for operations and controls. They are non-punitive and provide program guidance and criteria. Some include guidance for a self-audit. Many trade groups and other professional organizations have developed a range of guidelines and best practices for building organizational resilience. While best practices usually have superior results when applied and used as benchmarks, no one set of guidelines is always best for every organization.

To be truly effective, guidelines must be regularly revised to include newly improved practices. Here are some organizations that have developed guidelines:

→ The Disaster Recovery Institute International (DRII) developed *Professional Practices for Business Continuity Planners*, a set of ten best professional practices for business continuity and disaster recovery planning that provide a benchmark for business continuity practitioners. It is available for downloading at the DRII website: www.drii.org

→ The *Disaster Recovery Journal* (DRJ)—in collaboration with the Association of Records Management Administration (ARMA), DRII, the Financial Services Technology Consortium (FSTC), and the National Fire Protection Association (NFPA)— created the *Generally Accepted Practices for Business Continuity Practitioners (GAP)*. The effort also involved input from practitioners in all industries. *GAP* takes the best practice areas and adds definition and detail to the widely accepted ten professional competencies—BCP project initiation and management; risk evaluation and control; business impact analysis; developing BCP strategies; emergency response; developing and implementing the BCP; awareness and training; maintaining and exercising the BCP; public relations and crisis communications; and coordination with public authorities It is available for downloading at the DRJ website: www.drj.com

→ The Federal Financial Institutions Examination Council's (FFIEC)'s booklet *Business Continuity Planning* provides business continuity operating guidelines and guidance for examiners, financial institutions, and technology service providers to identify business continuity risks and evaluate controls and risk management practices for effective business continuity planning. It is available for downloading at the FFIEC website: www.ffiec.gov

→ The American Society for Industrial Security (ASIS) International publishes *Organizational Resilience: Security, Preparedness and Continuity Management Systems*, which provides auditable criteria to establish, check, maintain, and improve a program to manage disruptive events. It is available for purchase at the ASIS website: www.asisonline.org

→ The British Standards Institution (BSI), the national standards body of the United Kingdom, publishes BS-25999-Part 1, which provides best practice recommendations. A generic framework for continuity management and assistance in understanding the principles, process, and terminology of the business continuity management lifecycle, it is a guidance document only. It is available for purchase at the BSI website: bsigroup.com

→ The International Organization for Standardization (ISO) has published a new standard, ISO 31000-2009, which may result in looking at all risk management efforts, including business continuity, in a more inclusive way. ISO 31000-2009 was created by a working group representing twenty-eight countries and is a new international consensus standard that provides a broad framework for risk management. This framework is sufficiently generic to establish a common set of processes to manage risks throughout an organization. It is intended for use by all industries and business sectors and can be used by any public, private, or community enterprise, association, or group. The goal of the new voluntary standard is to make risk management fundamental to all key processes, including planning, management, and governance. It is intended to integrate and coordinate risk management processes in existing and future standards by providing a common approach in support of standards dealing with specific risks and/or business sectors. It is not intended to replace other standards. Though referred to as a standard, ISO 31000-2009 is really a set of guidelines and is not an accreditation or certification standard. It is available for purchase at the ISO website: www.iso.org

Standards

There is also increasing interest in establishing and using standards as guidance in developing and maintaining effective business continuity competency as well as to serve as a standardized guide in determining the quality and effectiveness of an organization's business continuity program. In this context, standards are typically formally approved precise criteria—policies, procedures, and instructions from recognized standards bodies such as the American National Standards Institute (ANSI) or the International Organization for Standardization (ISO). If an organization meets these voluntary standards, the reward is often in the form of a certification issued as evidence.

There has been somewhat of a rush to meet the need for standards. This has resulted in multiple sets of standards and benchmarks that have been or are currently being developed around the world—often with some accompanying turf wars. These are in addition to existing industry-specific standards. The new standards have the potential to be far-reaching in all business sectors. As a result, while sorting through the various voluntary guidelines and certification programs and mandatory regulations, there can be uncertainty in determining which to apply as the official yardstick in measuring internal efforts to develop and maintain an effective continuity program and in determining the continuity capability of the links in the supply chain.

Multiple standards that specifically detail or imply the need for business continuity planning have been developed by organizations throughout the world. These organizations and their published standards include:

→ The British Standards Institution (BSI): *BS-25999-2, 2007: Business Continuity Standards, Guidelines, and Voluntary Audit and Certification*

→ The National Fire Protection Association: *NFPA 1600-2010: Standard on Disaster/Emergency Management and Business Continuity Programs*

→ The International Organization for Standardization (ISO): *ISO/PAS 22399-2007, Societal Security: Guidelines for Incident Preparedness and Operational Continuity Management*, among other ISO standards that directly or indirectly address business continuity–related requirements

→ The Canadian Standards Association: *CSA Z1600, Standard for Emergency Management and Business Continuity Programs*

→ The Singapore Business Federation: *Singapore Standard SS540: 2008*, revised from *Technical Reference for Business Continuity*

→ The Private Sector–Department of Homeland Security Partnership: *Voluntary Private Sector Preparedness Accreditation and Certification Program (PS-Prep)*

Standards apply a carrot rather than a stick by conferring a certification on organizations that successfully meet the standards.

Voluntary Accreditation and Certification

The importance and influence of certification programs has increased significantly over the past several years. This creates the potential for the eventual development of a universal set of standards that can be applied when creating a business continuity program and to use in assessing the continuity capability of current critical supply chain partners as well as those under consideration for future contracts.

Today, organizations can voluntarily be audited and accredited against a choice of standards. As with any nonmandatory certification process, there are likely advantages for those who elect to utilize a certification standard. It behooves all businesses and organizations to stay informed and to consider which certification is of the greatest benefit to them, as well as which standard may be preferred in their industry or by their customers and clients. Two of the certification programs that are currently drawing significant attention are the British Standard BS-25999-2 and the Voluntary Private Sector Preparedness Accreditation and Certification Program (PS-Prep).

BS-25999-2 details specific requirements for developing, implementing, operating, monitoring, reviewing, exercising, maintaining, and improving a business continuity management system, taking into account an organization's overall business risks. The intent of the generic requirements is that they be applicable to all organizations, regardless of type or size. Application of the standards can be tailored to meet the needs of an organization, its customers, regulatory agencies, and all business and stakeholder requirements. They can be used within the organization or by external entities to assess the organization's capability to meet its internal continuity needs, as well as those of customers and other external stakeholders or other interested parties.

A successful audit by a third party enables an organization to demonstrate its compliance to the standard and be granted a certificate. Periodic monitoring and surveillance audits are required to validate continuing conformity to the requirements.

PS-Prep is among the newest standards. PS-Prep was mandated by Title IX of the Implementing Recommendations of the 9/11 Commission Act of 2007, directing the Department of Homeland Security (DHS) to develop and implement a voluntary program of accreditation and certification of private entities that promote private sector preparedness, including disaster management, emergency management, and business continuity programs. In July 2008, DHS announced an agreement with the ANSI-ASQ National Accreditation Board (ANAB). (The ANSI is the American National Standards Institute and the ASQ is the American Society for Quality.) The ANAB had been charged by DHS with developing, implementing, and administering an accreditation and certification program to meet the requirements of Title IX. The overriding goal is to improve private sector preparedness performance in disaster management, emergency management, and business continuity in order to enhance nationwide resilience. PS-Prep provides private entities with a methodology that will assist in effectively assessing the resilience of any organization, including critical supply chain links, as well as providing specific direction for developing an internal program.

Standards developed by the National Fire Protection Association (NFPA), the British Standards Institution (BSI), and the American Society for Industrial Security (ASIS) were selected as the basis for PS-Prep based on their scalability, balance of interest, and relevance to PS-Prep objectives. Under PS-Prep, recognition will be given to companies that have already completed preparedness measures as part of their regulatory audit process, to companies that have used existing recognized standards (such as NFPA 1600 and DRII's Ten Professional Practices) around which they have built their programs, and to companies that have used other accepted standards.

The aim of the voluntary program, intended for all businesses and organizations in the United States, is to allow for self-certification. A company that meets PS-Prep standards can issue a first-party attestation, a declaration certifying that the company is PS-Prep compliant. Organizations may be certified by an accredited third party establishing that the private sector entity conforms to one or more preparedness standards adopted by DHS. Expectations are that if PS-Prep is widely adopted as a business continuity standard, it can play a significant role in advancing supply chain resilience by providing a widely accepted vehicle for measuring continuity capability.

Weighing the Options

Certification is awarded to an organization that has adhered to a formal process and been assessed by an independent accredited third party that validates that the organization follows the principles set out in a standard and is therefore following industry best practices. Certification involves a comprehensive, documented validation of conformity to the requirements of a given standard and demonstrates that all elements of the standard have been addressed and met. Beyond the original certification process, there is a requirement for ongoing review to ensure that standard requirements are met in order to retain the certification.

For supply chain managers and procurement professionals, certifications can:

→ Simplify the process of validating suppliers' business continuity capability.
→ Provide a standard measure to compare potential suppliers and other business partners.
→ Serve as a supplier assessment program for organizations that have not yet developed one internally.

When an organization is the supplier or other business partner and needs to validate its capability to customers, or when an organization wants to establish and maintain a high level of continuity competency because it's good business to do so, a certification can:

→ Demonstrate the organization's commitment to business continuity.
→ Provide a means to provide all stakeholders and potential customers with a standardized validation of the continuity program.

→ Serve as a guide for developing and maintaining the internal business continuity program.

→ Result in possible insurance premium savings and credit rating enhancements.

While voluntary accreditation and certification programs can have significant benefits, there can be issues. If a supplier has multiple customers requesting certifications from different entities, the resulting need to be audited by and complete the paperwork required by multiple entities can become time- and cost-prohibitive. For example, PS-Prep is a U.S. standard, BS-25999 is a British standard, and neither is as yet a globally accepted standard. A global enterprise may find it difficult to determine which will better serve its needs.

There is also some pushback from businesses that believe that the last thing needed is an additional audit, even when it is associated with a voluntary program. In light of the expense and effort U.S. businesses experienced surrounding the Sarbanes-Oxley Act of 2002, this is perhaps understandable. (The Sarbanes-Oxley Act established a broad range of standards for public companies, their boards, and accounting firms.)

Organizations may hesitate to adopt any standard-based voluntary certification program until the dust has settled and there is full consensus, or at least a reasonable level of agreement, as to which of the available standards (or one yet to be released) will be the most widely accepted. As these are voluntary standards, there is no penalty for not complying, allowing leeway to wait and see how the situation unfolds and to more fully measure the value and acceptance of the available certification programs. Yet once customers begin mandating that current suppliers show continuity competency by means of a certification, or once certification becomes a requirement to submit a proposal, it is no longer truly voluntary. The marketplace becomes the driver.

There are potential gains and losses for all the entities involved. Individuals can be certified to audit programs for certification, companies can develop and deliver related training, and certifying bodies with the most widely accepted accreditation and certification programs can gain greater control and income. Accreditation should not serve as a stimulus package for consultants, trainers, publishers, and certifying organizations. The focus should be on how all organizations can become better prepared to face the challenges of operational disruptions and disasters.

Ultimately, it must be understood that even fully meeting the requirements for certification does not necessarily spell success for a business continuity program. To succeed in the real world and not just on paper, business continuity must be incorporated into the organization's policies, day-to-day operations, and culture.

Professional Certification

Certification as a means of credentialing individuals involved in a given profession has been around since the 1920s. It is a widely accepted way to validate knowledge and skills in a given profession or activity and serves multiple purposes. For employers and clients, certification validates the individual's professional quality standards, knowledge, and experience, as well as ongoing efforts to update skills and access the most current ideas through continuing education. Certifying organizations prescribe both a code of professional ethics and the use of approved methodologies that provide guidance to the practitioner and confidence to the employer. For the individual, certification offers recognition of professional achievement and the possibility of career enhancement.

Options for certifications to validate skills and experience in the field have increased, and each certification has an accompanying acronym. Chief among the organizations awarding certifications are:

→ The Disaster Recovery Institute International (DRII), which awards several levels of business continuity and disaster recovery planning certification

→ The International Association of Emergency Managers (IAEM), which confers the Certified Emergency Manager (CEM) and Associate Emergency Manager (AEM) designations

→ The Business Continuity Institute (BCI), which has a multiple-level certification program

There are both similarities and significant differences in the certification philosophy and methodology for measuring competency and awarding a credential:

→ DRII provides multiple levels of professional certifications. These certifications, which acknowledge an effort to achieve a professional level of competence in the industry, include an Associate Business Continuity Professional (ABCP), a Certified Business Continuity Professional (CBCP), and a Master Business Continuity Professional (MBCP). More recently, other classifications have been added to certify business continuity vendors as well as audit options. Certification is a two-part process: (1) verification of knowledge by a grade of 75 percent or higher on a written examination, and (2) an extensive written application that outlines professional experience that is reviewed by a panel of professionals and confirmed. Maintaining certification requires the submission of approved continuing education activity points every two years.

→ IAEM offers an Associate Emergency Manager (AEM) and a Certified Emergency Manager (CEM) designation for qualified professionals with comprehensive emergency management experience in the areas of mitigation, preparedness, response, and recovery for all risks. Applicants for the CEM designation must validate a minimum of three years of relevant experience, have earned a college degree, demonstrate contributions to the profession, write an essay, and pass a multiple-choice examination. While AEM certification requires passing an exam and writing an essay, the professional experience and education requirements are less rigorous. Certification maintenance includes documented points in three categories: education and instruction, professional participation, and service and leadership.

→ The BCI bases its certification on the knowledge gained through professional experience. All applicants for professional-certified grades—such as the Associate Member (AMBCI), Specialist Member (SBCI), and Member (MBCI)—are required to pass an examination that verifies the applicant's knowledge of the BCI's Good Practice Guidelines and to complete a scored-assessment matrix, listing their applicable experience in each of ten business continuity disciplines. This information is validated by the applicant's references. A recently added BCI program extends eligibility for BCI membership to professionals who hold certain certifications from other industry associations (such as the DRII's MBCP, CBCP, or ABCP), and have the required length of business continuity management experience. Under this program, there is no requirement to pass the BCI's official exam. The BCI Fellow certification—leading to the designation of FBCI—is reserved for those with a minimum of six years experience as a business continuity practitioner. Candidates for the Fellow designation must demonstrate that they have made a significant contribution to the advancement of the profession beyond performing a job—such as sharing their knowledge and experience with others through writing, teaching, or public speaking—or in some other way furthered the profession. The BCI requires no recertification as long as the certified professional continues to work in business continuity and adheres to the BCI Code of Practice, the professional standards required by the Institute as a condition of membership.

Employers or clients are assured that the credentialed individual has the education, training, knowledge base, experience, and dedication to the profession to qualify him or her to perform at a specified level of competency. Consideration of a candidate's certification is a valuable component in the overall selection process when you are hiring an employee to assume business continuity responsibilities or contracting with a consultant to assist with a continuity planning project.

Going Forward

Business continuity reflects a concern for improving the capacity to respond to, recover from, and fully resume operations after extreme events. Any set of guidelines or standards has a rather broad charge when seeking to establish one way for all organizations to approach business continuity planning and perhaps overlapping disaster recovery and emergency preparedness. There will always be disagreement about which organization provides the most effective benchmark and which standard gives the most accurate measurement of an organization's capability to meet the challenges of disasters that disrupt operations.

It behooves each business and organization to be informed of the evolving situation with continuity guidelines and standards and to consider whether following a set of accepted standards meets the company's needs. When making the decision, continue to evaluate what will result in the greatest benefit and whether the selected standards or certification is the best vehicle for continually improving continuity capability.

→ Research to learn whether there are any government regulations that require your organization to maintain a business continuity program.

→ Determine whether there is a business continuity standard that is preferred or recommended by your organization's industry or profession.

→ Ascertain whether key customers or clients have selected guidelines or a standard to apply to their continuity planning.

→ Explore the pluses and minuses of obtaining accreditation and certification through one of the currently available voluntary programs.

→ Determine whether it is in the best interests of your organization to request that your suppliers and other business partners obtain certification.

Business Continuity Planning Assessment Questionnaire

Use the following survey to assess your organization's current level of business continuity preparedness. For each statement, circle the score from 1 to 5 that you believe best reflects what is in place today, 1 being the lowest score, 5 being the highest score (1 = nothing currently in place; 5 = fully implemented). Note: If you do not know whether something exists, for purposes of this assessment, it does not.

	Low				High
Section 1. Business Continuity Program					
Our company has an organization-wide business continuity program.	1	2	3	4	5
There are company policies that set forth business continuity standards.	1	2	3	4	5
A designated business continuity planning group addresses all business continuity issues.	1	2	3	4	5
The organization has a business continuity manager or other individual assigned specific, ongoing responsibility for our business continuity program.	1	2	3	4	5
Auditors, a business continuity consultant, or other outside independent reviews the program annually.	1	2	3	4	5

We have developed and adopted standardized business continuity terminology used throughout the organization.   1 2 3 4 5

We have an essential records program that includes established retention cycles and off-site storage of all critical documents (electronic, paper, microfiche, etc.).   1 2 3 4 5

Business continuity responsibilities are assigned to each department.   1 2 3 4 5

Our organization has emergency provisions in place that include management succession plans.   1 2 3 4 5

All electronic data files are backed up daily and backups are stored at an off-site location.   1 2 3 4 5

Section 1 Score: _____

Section 2. Supply Chain Business Continuity

All supply chain business units are fully included in the business continuity planning process.   1 2 3 4 5

At least one representative of the supply chain business units is a member of the business continuity planning group.   1 2 3 4 5

Existing plans include business continuity procedures and strategies for supply chain business units.   1 2 3 4 5

Supplier business continuity capability is included in our procurement selection process.   1 2 3 4 5

We review and document our supply chain risks and threats on an annual basis.   1 2 3 4 5

Our department maintains an up-to-date list of contact information for all suppliers, contractors, and shippers.   1 2 3 4 5

A list of key people and qualified alternates for each key person needed for critical business functions is maintained.   1 2 3 4 5

A list of critical suppliers and an alternate for each is maintained and updated at least twice annually.   1 2 3 4 5

Section 2 Score: _____

Section 3. Security, Facilities, and Life Safety Systems

Our building is equipped with life safety systems   1 2 3 4 5
including emergency lighting, a fire suppression
system, fire extinguishers, and a fire alarm system.

We have trained employee Emergency Response   1 2 3 4 5
Teams who assist and help evacuate employees
and others when an emergency or disaster occurs.

Our organization maintains and regularly inventories 1 2 3 4 5
and updates emergency supplies and equipment.

We have physical security measures in place that   1 2 3 4 5
include building access controls.

Section 3 Score: _____

Section 4. Training and Awareness

Employee orientation and refresher training in life   1 2 3 4 5
safety and security procedures (e.g., evacuation, bomb
threats, medical emergencies) is conducted regularly.

All employees are familiar with our emergency   1 2 3 4 5
contact procedures.

Employee orientation and refresher training is   1 2 3 4 5
conducted in business continuity procedures.

We have an established schedule of business   1 2 3 4 5
continuity training, tests, and exercises.

Section 4 Score: _____

Section 5. Business Continuity — Your Perspective

I am confident that our company is adequately   1 2 3 4 5
prepared to handle unplanned business interruptions.

I am aware of what my role is should the company   1 2 3 4 5
experience a disaster.

I have received sufficient business continuity training. 1 2 3 4 5

I have read the business continuity plan.   1 2 3 4 5

I keep a current list of company emergency contact   1 2 3 4 5
numbers with me at all times.

Section 5 Score: _____

Add up the scores for each section. Transfer the score from each section. Then add the section totals for an overall total score.

1. Business Continuity Program _____/50
2. Supply Chain Business Continuity _____/40
3. Security, Facilities, and Life Safety Systems _____/20
4. Training and Awareness _____/20
5. Business Continuity—Your Perspective _____/25
TOTAL OVERALL SCORE _____/155

Interpreting Your Score

155 Outstanding. Continue to maintain and update the program regularly.

125–154 Excellent job. Identify the areas needing further enhancement; continue updates and testing and training. Strive to embed business continuity in the organization's culture.

95–124 A good start. Note sections with lowest scores; concentrate efforts there.

65–94 Considerable improvement is needed. Choose two or three items as first steps. Attempt to gain greater executive support for the program.

0–64 There is a great deal of work to be done. Get started now. Develop a comprehensive project plan; involve people from all areas of the organization. Find an executive sponsor for the project.

APPENDIX *B*

General and Supply Chain–Specific Hazards

Hazard Identification—General

While not by any means all-inclusive, the following is a partial list of general risks and threats that may impact an organization's facilities or operations, either directly or indirectly. The list includes natural, technological, and human-caused threats. While any of these threats can interfere with the supply chain operations, they are threats to the entire enterprise and not specific to the supply chain.

→ Avalanche
→ Bomb explosion
→ Bomb threat
→ Communications system failure (phone, cell phone)
→ Cyber attack, hacking, computer virus, etc.
→ Earthquake
→ Electrical storm
→ Employee fraud
→ Equipment breakdown
→ Explosion

→ Fire caused by arson
→ Fire caused by lightning
→ Fire from other cause
→ Flood
→ Hazardous material incident (internal or external source)
→ Human error
→ Hurricane
→ HVAC failure
→ Ice storm
→ IT failure
→ Labor action (strike, work stoppage or slowdown)
→ Loss of key employees
→ Natural gas supply interruption
→ Nuclear accident
→ Pandemic (SARS, H1N1, etc.)
→ Plane crash
→ Political upheaval
→ Power outage or brownout
→ Regulatory noncompliance
→ Riot/public demonstration
→ Sabotage (internal or external source)
→ Security breach
→ Severe winter storm
→ Skilled labor shortage
→ Terrorism
→ Theft of property (internal or external perpetrator)
→ Theft of trade secrets or intellectual property
→ Tornado
→ Transportation accident (air, highway, pipeline, rail, water)
→ Tsunami
→ Violence in the workplace
→ Volcanic eruption
→ Wastewater service interruption

→ Water supply interruption

→ Wild land fire

Hazard Identification—Supply Chain–Specific

The supply chain is at risk from all the previously listed threats. In addition, the following is a partial list of supply chain–specific risks and threats that directly impact the supply chain and its links. While these have an impact beyond the supply chain, the direct impact is on supply chain operations. Again, this is not an all-inclusive list.

→ Failure of tier suppliers

→ Import or export delay

→ Logistics disruptions and delay

→ Pirate attack

→ Political instability

→ Product shrinkage during shipping

→ Product tampering

→ Production problems (internal)

→ Supplier going out of business (bankruptcy or other cause)

→ Supplier quality breakdown

→ Supply chain security break

→ Supply shortage (components, parts, materials)

→ Transportation disruption (highways, waterways, air, railways)

→ Volatile costs (commodities, labor, transportation, energy)

Pandemic Planning

The World Health Organization (WHO) has established six pandemic phases and related threat levels. (See Figure C-1.) This threat phase approach is similar to the Department of Homeland Security's five terrorist threat levels.

Planning assumptions that are reasonable to use when developing plans to address a possible pandemic should include the following:

→ Remedies will not necessarily be readily available and may be in very limited supply; those in professions deemed critical, such as first responders and healthcare workers, will have first priority.

→ It is not unreasonable to expect a 30 percent to 40 percent, and perhaps even as high as 50 percent, absenteeism rate, not only among employees but also among contractors, suppliers, consultants, and community service and public safety workers.

→ Absenteeism may also result from fear or the need to care for children and/or elderly family members.

→ There may be erratic delivery of goods and services provided by suppliers, contractors, outsourcing companies, and consultants.

→ A pandemic may last as long as eighteen months in waves.

→ Gathering places such as shopping areas, schools, events, conference centers, and sports arenas will be closed.

FIGURE C-1.

PANDEMIC PHASES.

Inter-pandemic phase	Low risk of human cases	1
New virus in animals, no human cases	Higher risk of human cases	2
Pandemic alert	No or very limited human-to-human transmission	3
New virus causes human cases	Evidence of increased human-to-human transmission	4
	Evidence of significant human-to-human transmission	5
Pandemic	Efficient and sustained human-to-human transmission	6

Source: World Health Organization.

→ Even if an employee population is healthy, a state or local agency could issue and enforce a quarantine that would last an undetermined length of time.

→ Based on the severity and breadth of a pandemic, travel could be limited or prohibited into and out of impacted areas.

Suggested actions include a wide range of strategies from stocking masks and gloves, to using videoconferencing rather than have employees travel to meetings, to developing plans to move employees to alternate work sites and developing the capability to have employees work from home.

As an initial step, establish with executive officers or the board what level of business activity they expect during a pandemic, be it business as usual or severely reduced operations. This information provides a benchmark for pandemic planning.

Establish a high-level planning group, including representation from the executive group, whose members can quickly make decisions and take immediate action if required to respond to pandemic threats.

Initiate or continue a program to train employees on how

to help prevent the spread of germs and how to prepare their homes and families.

Some steps can be taken immediately to prepare, including the following:

→ Review business continuity plans for adequacy to respond to extreme numbers of employee absences.

→ Create checklists for each functional area of the company by pandemic phase. Create policies addressing visitors, travel, and compensation.

→ Develop a communications plan specifically for use should a pandemic occur.

→ Conduct tabletop exercises using a pandemic scenario.

→ Provide training for employees to help them prepare at home.

→ Keep executives briefed on progress of the planning and on updated pandemic information as it becomes available.

→ Develop an annex or a stand-alone section of the business continuity plan specifically to cover the pandemic threat.

→ Create a work-from-home strategy in the event quarantine is declared.

→ Determine whether suppliers, contractors, and other business partners have adequate pandemic response plans.

Possible additional actions for the immediate future might include:

→ Make sure that succession plans are adequate and current.

→ If not already in place, consider setting up work-at-home capabilities for the most time-critical employees. Supply them with necessary equipment and supplies, and install alternative broadband services at their residences.

→ Make web conferencing available to customers, suppliers, contractors, all business locations, and time-critical employees.

→ Develop redundancies in the event there are network outages.

→ Clean or change HVAC filters regularly; check manufacturer's recommendations and make sure that what is currently being done is not less than that recommended.

→ Have kitchens and restrooms cleaned more frequently; check with cleaning staff or contractors to be certain they are using disinfectants.

A fully developed business continuity plan will likely cover many of these steps such as alternate work site, disaster communications capabilities, and determining supply chain preparedness.

Each threat level higher than Phase 3 signals the need for a review of the pandemic plan and the need for additional steps. Here are supplementary action lists specifically for pandemic threat Phase 4, Phase 5, and Phase 6.

Pandemic Phase 4—Evidence of Increased Human-to-Human Transmission

→ Develop and implement process for monitoring absences due to illness, and provide regular reports to the pandemic planning group.

→ Contact local public safety officials to become familiar with local preparedness measures.

→ Communicate to your employee population that the company has developed a planned response for responding to a pandemic should the company be directly impacted.

→ Develop special pandemic employee policies:

  → For paying employees who (1) are ill, (2) are needed at home to care for ill household members, (3) must stay at home to care for children due to forced or voluntary closures of schools and/or child care centers, (4) are afraid of possible exposure, (5) have no transportation, or (6) experience losses.

  → For paying employees should it be necessary to temporarily shut down a facility.

  → For limiting or discontinuing travel.

  → Stay-at-home requirement for employees returning from an infected area.

→ Review your employee assistance program to ensure availability of employee counseling should it be required.

→ Explore additional work-from-home capabilities.

→ Consider the impact of the pandemic on your supply chain and what additional pre-planning is necessary.

→ Require additional cross-training for functions identified as highly time-critical.

→ Request that cleaning crews clean nonporous services such as light switches and elevator buttons with a disinfectant solution and periodically use a disinfectant spray on chairs and desks.

→ Monitor to ensure that kitchens and restrooms are cleaned regularly with disinfectant and that HVAC filters are regularly cleaned or changed in accordance with the manufacturer's recommendations.

→ Provide training and written material for employees on how to prepare at home.

→ Ensure that key vendors and contractors have sufficient pandemic planning in place. As necessary, plan for alternate source for services and products.

→ Develop policies addressing visitors to offices, warehouses, and other facilities such as limiting or prohibiting access.

→ Determine if additional items should be addressed in an escalation plan, based on existing conditions and level of risk.

Pandemic Phase 5—Evidence of Significant Human-to-Human Transmission

→ Establish minimum staffing requirements for all locations.

→ Develop closing and reopening procedures for locations where acceptable staffing levels cannot be accomplished and/or where local officials order forced closings.

→ Use teleconferencing and video conferencing rather than in-person meetings between locations whenever possible.

→ Establish a comprehensive public relations plan to implement should it be necessary to close offices, manufacturing plants, warehouses, or other facilities.

→ Consider adjusting inventory levels.

Pandemic Phase 6—Efficient and Sustained Human-to-Human Transmission

→ Implement daily updates to outgoing messages on emergency phone lines or emergency notification systems to provide current status information to employees and others.

→ Check staffing daily; implement closing procedures for locations with insufficient staffing or where local authorities have ordered forced closings.

The Business Continuity Team

Once continuity strategies are developed, people are needed to enact and carry out the procedures that are detailed in the plan documents. A predefined business continuity team's purpose is to manage resources with a goal of continuing or resuming operations following a disaster. People and their skills, equipment, supplies, physical space, information, financial resources, and supply chain links must be coordinated and focused on the goals and objectives of the business continuity plan.

To quote the late W. Alton Jones, the oil executive responsible for completing oil pipelines from Texas to the East Coast, "The man who gets the most satisfactory results is not always the man with the most brilliant single mind, but rather the man who can best coordinate the brains and talents of his associates." Someone must manage and coordinate the efforts of those responsible for carrying out the business continuity plan. For each of the organization's continuity teams, the team leader is responsible for directing team members and communicating and coordinating with other teams.

In organizations with a business continuity coordinator and program, it is likely that the continuity team organization and the reporting structure have been established. If a supply chain continuity team or teams are being added to the continuity organization, the existing structure is used with adjustments to accommodate supply chain–specific continuity requirements.

Team Models

The size and complexity of the business, its product or service, and whether it is a corporation, a not-for-profit organization, or a government agency are among the deciding factors when determining the most suitable continuity team structure. Just as there is no one-size-fits-all business continuity plan, no one team structure is best for every organization. Consider these five team models that are based on actual business continuity teams. With some tailoring, one of them, or a combination of two or more of them, may be the continuity structure that is best suited to meet the needs of your organization.

1. Functional units team model
2. Alternate functional units team model
3. Incident Command System (ICS) model
4. Technical teams model
5. Corporate business continuity team model

After reviewing the models, decide which model, adjusted model, or combination of models is the best fit for your organization and its business continuity strategies. If you currently have a team structure in place, you will likely find that one of these models is the same or similar to your organization's continuity team configuration.

Model 1: Functional Units Team Model

The functional units team model (shown in Figure D-1) loosely reflects the company's organization chart with a team representing each department or major business unit. Team leads report to the organization's business continuity manager, who reports to the corporate continuity team or executive group.

FUNCTIONAL UNITS TEAM MODEL.

Model 2: Alternate Functional Units Team Model

In this model (shown in Figure D-2), business units are grouped by category such as administration, facilities, supply chain, technical services, financial, and operations, with a representative of each group of departments serving as the team lead. In the example shown in Figure D-2, team leads report to the business continuity manager who, in turn, reports to the corporate business continuity team.

Model 3: Incident Command System (ICS) Model

First used by the fire service, the Incident Command System (ICS) is endorsed by the Federal Emergency Management Agency (FEMA) and has become the standard for emergency management across the United States. It is used by emergency management organizations, lifeline organizations, and government agencies at all levels in Continuity of Operation (COOP) plans (the term used by government agencies to fulfill the requirement that all agencies have in place a viable capability that ensures the performance of their essential functions during any emergency or situation that may disrupt normal operations) and others that coordinate with public agencies at the time of a disaster. ICS is also being adopted by some businesses.

When multiple entities are jointly involved in managing

FIGURE D-2.

ALTERNATE FUNCTIONAL UNITS TEAM MODEL.

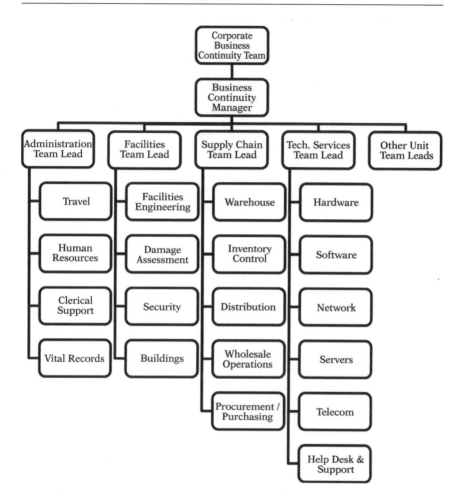

a disaster, having the same organizational structure facilitates more effective command, control, coordination, and communication. In Figure D-3, note the four sections—operations, planning, logistics, and finance—as well as the support positions: liaison, public information officer (PIO), and safety officer. These are the standard functions in an ICS organization.

INCIDENT COMMAND SYSTEM (ICS) MODEL.

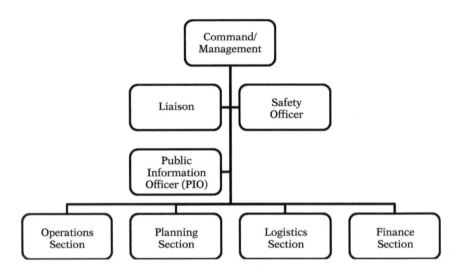

Model 4: Technical Teams Model

This model (shown in Figure D-4) is most often used for disaster recovery teams and by companies whose business is technology-driven. Each team has a team leader who reports to the business continuity manager or disaster recovery manager.

Model 5: Corporate Business Continuity Team Model

This model (shown in Figure D-5) is primarily used by very large corporations and organizations that have an enterprise-wide business continuity program. Each business unit or department has a department business continuity team. One of the teams is the IT department's disaster recovery team. There is a full-time business continuity planning manager and a corporate business continuity team coordinator, as well as a position whose sole responsibility is to be the liaison between

TECHNICAL TEAMS MODEL.

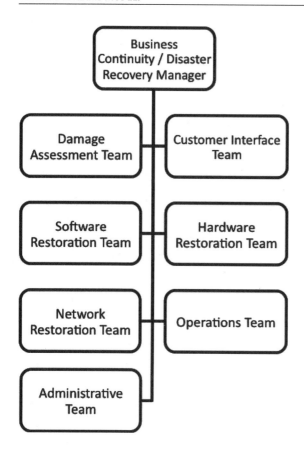

the business continuity team coordinator and the executive group. The leader of each of the teams—such as operations, facilities, and finance—reports to the corporate business continuity team coordinator. Based on the organization, other business unit teams might include human resources, communications, regulatory and legal, or information security. The business continuity planning manager acts as an observer to identify needed improvements and is available to advise and assist the corporate business continuity team coordinator.

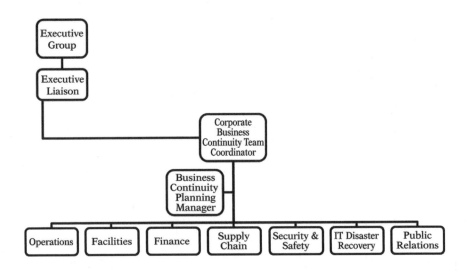

FIGURE D-5.

CORPORATE BUSINESS CONTINUITY TEAM MODEL.

Assigning Roles and Responsibilities

Regardless of the continuity team structure, one primary person and two backups should be assigned to each position on the team. This helps eliminate the possibility of unfilled positions when the primary person assigned to a position is unavailable for any reason and makes it possible for team members to work in shifts when the continuity effort must operate on a 24/7 basis.

Business continuity team members may or may not be the same people who served as members of the business continuity planning group. Make certain that those individuals who make up the continuity team have the necessary knowledge, skills, and experience necessary to manage the disaster and carry out the plan. Equally important is that they be given the authority, responsibility, and tools necessary for them to succeed.

There are several things to take into account when appointing team members. Team members must understand the organization and how it functions to be able to restore it following a disaster. Assets and capabilities that make effective team leaders include decisiveness, willingness to delegate, the ability to see the big picture, and having credibility with management and team members. Beyond functional skill sets, individuals who are creative, flexible, reasonable risk takers, can remain calm in challenging situations, and are people-oriented make excellent business continuity team members. Two other traits that are invaluable for all team members are a sense of humor and common sense.

Business Continuity Center

Teams require a location from which to manage the continuity effort. When the usual work location is habitable, accessible, and has infrastructure support, the team will likely use a conference room or other large space in the building as its business continuity center.

If the primary work location is not habitable or accessible, the team must operate from a pre-identified alternate location such as a leased workspace center, another company facility, or perhaps a business partner's facility. Organizations have even located business continuity centers in hotel meeting rooms and conference centers. Just as with team staffing, best practices call for having one primary location and two backup locations. Wherever the business continuity center is located, coordinate with the security department to ensure that necessary security measures are in place and that access is controlled.

The business continuity center must be properly equipped with copies of the plan, checklists, logs, forms, whiteboards to track progress, and perhaps blueprints, operating manuals, or maps. Communications equipment and computers are necessary. A radio and television are helpful in monitoring media reports about natural disasters or a disaster that is specific to the organization and gains media attention. Current phone directories are a valuable resource for locating needed supplies, equipment, or services.

Continuity Plan Samples

The first of the following three sample documents is a table of contents for a corporate business continuity plan. The second is an example of one that might be used for a department or other business unit plan. The final document is a sample basic plan for a department or other business unit.

Sample Table of Contents for a Corporate Business Continuity Plan

PART 4: DEACTIVATION

PART 5: ATTACHMENTS

Sample Table of Contents for a Department or Business Unit Continuity Plan

Plan Distribution List
Record of Plan Changes and Revisions
Glossary

PART I: INTRODUCTION

1.1   Compliance with Corporate Business Continuity Policies and Standards
1.2   Time Requirements
1.3   Continuity Activities
    1.3.1   First 8 Hours
    1.3.2   First 24 Hours
    1.3.3   24–72 Hours
    1.3.4   Days 3–7
1.4   Department/Business Unit Business Continuity Team
1.5   Business Continuity Team Location
1.6   Coordination with Business Continuity Organization

PART 2: POLICIES AND PROCEDURES

2.1   Activation and Notification
2.2   Situation Assessment
2.3   Business Continuity Team Initial Briefing
2.4   Continuity Priorities
2.5   Restoration Time Frames
2.6   Continuity Strategies and Procedures
    2.6.1   Relocation
    2.6.2   Temporary Suspension
    2.6.3   Contracted and Outsourced Services
2.7   Situation Tracking
2.8   Employee Information
2.9   Long-Term Recovery
2.10 Tracking Continuity Costs
2.11 Department Continuity Strategies
    2.11.1   Asset Protection
    2.11.2   Vital Records Protection and Reconstruction
    2.11.3   Essential Systems and Applications
    2.11.4   Resource Needs
    2.11.5   Staffing and Scheduling
    2.11.6   Notification and Recall
    2.11.7   Business Continuity Procedures

2.12   Deactivation Procedures

2.13   Training and Testing

2.14   Plan Review and Revision

PART 3: ATTACHMENTS

A.   Department Business Continuity Team Members and Contact Information

B.   Relocation Logistics

    B.1   Directions and Map

    B.2   Relocation Site Contact Information

    B.3   Reporting Procedures

    B.4   Alternate Work Area Set-Up Instructions

    B.5   Approved Area Hotels

    B.6   Area Restaurants

C.   Business Continuity Organization and Contact Information

D.   Department Detailed Business Continuity Procedures

E.   Alternate Communications Procedures

F.   Sample Status Report Form

G.   Sample Regulatory Compliance Form

H.   Department Employee Contact List

I.   Sample Expense Reporting Form

J.   Department Resource Needs List

K.   Supplier/Vendor/Contractor Contact List

L.   Business Continuity Action Checklists

NOTE: Other attachments may include but are not limited to:

    Product Flow Charts

    Process Flow Charts

    Work-Around Procedures

    Floor and Site Layouts

    Alternate Shipping Routes, Maps, and Directions

    Organization Charts (such as other departments, divisions, supply chain business partners)

Company Name	Department/Business Unit Name
Logo	Sample Business Continuity Plan

Sample Basic Plan for a Department or Business Unit Continuity Plan

[NAME OF DEPARTMENT/BUSINESS UNIT] Business Continuity Plan

1.0 INTRODUCTION

With a goal of minimizing the impact of possible business disasters, the *XYZ Corporation* has developed and implemented an enterprise-wide Business Continuity Program. The goal of the program is to ensure the company's capability to continue or restore essential business operations following a natural, technological, or incited disaster.

Under the executive sponsorship of our *Executive Vice President* and the leadership of the *Business Continuity Manager*, a Business Continuity Program has been developed and tested that will allow continuation or restoration of all identified time-critical business functions.

The purpose of the *department/business unit's* Business Continuity Plan (BCP) is to provide guidance and instructions for restoring the department's time-critical business functions following any major disruption. The goal of this plan in coordination with the Corporate Business Continuity Program is resumption of normal business operations and services as soon as possible following any disaster. Business Continuity Plans will be activated following events of any type that interrupt normal business operations.

This plan is in full compliance with all Corporate business continuity policies, standards, and guidelines and applicable legal and regulatory requirements.

A separate Disaster Recovery Plan developed by the Information Technology (IT) Department provides for restoration of essential

(Name of Dept. or Business Unit) Business Continuity Plan File Path (C:\Administrator\ MyDocuments\.......)

Date of Last Revision: 0-00-00

Basic Plan: Page 1 of 22

Company Name	Department/Business Unit Name
Logo	Sample Business Continuity Plan

---

data systems and applications needed to support time-critical business functions following a disruption.

Business Continuity Plan staffing takes into account that some department employees may not be available at the time a disaster occurs and to the extent possible provides for backups for all Business Continuity Team members and employees assigned continuity responsibilities.

1.1 COMPLIANCE WITH CORPORATE BUSINESS CONTINUITY POLICIES AND STANDARDS

This plan complies fully with *XYZ Corporation*'s business continuity standards and is in compliance with all related policies. This plan coordinates with the Corporate Business Continuity Plan's all *business unit/department* Business Continuity Plans.

In implementing and carrying out this plan, personal safety will always be the first priority. While our company's business continuity plans are developed and maintained in accordance with current best practices, nothing in this plan should preclude or override the exercise of prudent judgment and common sense based on the specific situation and conditions during disaster conditions.

XYZ Corporation's Business Continuity Program and all Business Continuity Plans are designed to prepare for significant business disruptions and to enable *XYZ Corporation* to rapidly resume our business operations as quickly as possible if an event does occur. As this plan and all related plans are applicable to many different emergency and disaster situations and as these events are unpredictable by their very nature, it is not possible to anticipate every possible situation that can impact

---

(Name of Dept. or Business Unit) Business Continuity Plan File Path (C:\Administrator\ MyDocuments\.......)

Date of Last Revision: 0-00-00

Basic Plan: Page 2 of 22

our ability to conduct business, nor is it possible to foretell the actual conditions we may experience in an actual disaster situation. As a result, business continuity teams will have to be flexible in responding to actual events as they occur.

1.2 TIME REQUIREMENTS

The IT Department's Disaster Recovery Plan includes a goal of restoration of time-critical data and communications systems within not more than 72 hours of the declaration of a disaster. To synchronize with this goal, the *department/business unit's* Business Continuity Plan will enable the department to continue its time-critical business functions without IT support for up to 72 hours.

1.3 CONTINUITY ACTIVITIES

The specific restoration activities to be undertaken will be dictated by the presenting situation and its impact on employees, facilities, utilities, and normal business operations. Generally speaking, the focus of business continuity activities will center on the following priorities and time frames.

1.3.1 First 8 Hours

- → Personnel—life safety
- → All notifications (internal and external)
- → Damage assessment and containment
- → Security issues
- → Communications (internal and external)

Company Name   Department/Business Unit Name
Logo   Sample Business Continuity Plan

- → Activation of all *department/business unit* Business Continuity Teams
- → Evolving and changing situation
- → Ongoing situation assessment

1.3.2 First 24 Hours

- → Full implementation of all business continuity plans and procedures
- → Review all restoration priorities and strategies and adjust as required
- → Restore and repair voice and data networks
- → Based on business cycles, identify most immediate recovery objectives for time-sensitive functions and adjust priorities as required
- → Obtain resources needed to restore time-critical business functions
- → Communications (internal and external)
- → Update *department/business unit*'s employees on status

1.3.3 24–72 Hours

- → Relocate to and configure alternate location, if required
- → Restore time-critical business functions
- → Delay/suspend nonessential business functions

(Name of Dept. or Business Unit) Business Continuity Plan File Path (C:\Administrator\ MyDocuments\.......)

Date of Last Revision: 0-00-00

Basic Plan: Page 4 of 22

→ Communications (internal and external)

→ Update *department/business unit*'s employees on status

1.3.4 Days 3–7

→ Reassess the disaster's impact and current status

→ Determine estimated duration of any disruptions

→ Identify restoration strategies and schedule for long-term restoration of non–time-critical business functions

→ Establish personnel schedules

→ Communications (internal and external)

→ Update *department/business unit*'s employees on status

1.4 *(DEPARTMENT/BUSINESS UNIT)* BUSINESS CONTINUITY TEAM

The *title of person* will serve as the *department/business unit*'s Business Continuity Team Leader (BCT Leader) unless she or he is unavailable or delegates that responsibility. Should the *Team Leader's title* be unavailable, the responsibilities of BCT Leader will be assumed by the *title of alternate person*.

The *department/business unit*'s BCT leader will have leadership responsibility for implementing the *department/business unit*'s Business Continuity Plan with a goal of continuation of the department's time-critical business functions and restora-

---

(Name of Dept. or Business
Unit) Business Continuity Plan
File Path (C:\Administrator\
MyDocuments\.......)

Date of Last Revision: 0-00-00

Basic Plan: Page 5 of 22

tion of normal business activities. To ensure required business continuity staffing, the *department/business unit's* Business Continuity Team is comprised of a primary and two backups for each team position. To the extent possible all department personnel are trained to carry out all critical business functions.

Primary Team Member	1st Backup	2nd Backup
Team Leader		

All Business Continuity Team members will participate in two training sessions, two tabletop exercises, and one functional exercise annually.

Department/business unit's BCT members are encouraged to maintain some basic personal supplies at the workplace to include toilet articles such as toothpaste, toothbrush, and any medications they might need. BCT members should have a plan for contacting their family and relatives in the event that they are unable to return home on schedule. It is also recommended that they designate an out-of-state relative or friend that they and their family members can contact to coordinate messages.

Department/business unit's BCT members and their contact information are listed in Attachment A to this plan. The BCT

(Name of Dept. or Business Unit) Business Continuity Plan File Path (C:\Administrator\ MyDocuments\.......)

Date of Last Revision: 0-00-00

Basic Plan: Page 6 of 22

Company Name	Department/Business Unit Name
Logo	Sample Business Continuity Plan

Team Leader is responsible for a quarterly update of Attachment A.

1.5 BUSINESS CONTINUITY TEAM LOCATION

Upon notification of a significant disruption to operations, the Business Continuity Team (BCT) will convene at the *(primary work location such as office, distribution center, warehouse)* if feasible. If the building is damaged or inaccessible, the BCT will convene at either *(alternate location such as another company facility or contracted alternate work area site)*.

Should any BCT member not be at his/her usual workplace or unable to reach the *alternate location,* he/she will attempt to communicate status and location via *preestablished communications methods.*

Attachment B contains relocation logistics such as basic information about the alternate work area sites, addresses, maps, and access process.

1.6 COORDINATION WITH BC ORGANIZATION

As an integral part of the company's Business Continuity organization, the *department/business unit's* Business Continuity Plan is in compliance with all *XYZ Corporation's* Business Continuity policies and standards. The *department/business unit's* BCT will coordinate with the Corporate Business Continuity Team and all other company Department Business Continuity Teams and participate in all planning activities, training, exercises, and tests as required. Attachment C details the company's business continuity organization.

(Name of Dept. or Business Unit) Business Continuity Plan File Path (C:\Administrator\ MyDocuments\.......)

Date of Last Revision: 0-00-00

Basic Plan: Page 7 of 22

Company Name	Department/Business Unit Name
Logo	Sample Business Continuity Plan

2.0 POLICIES AND PROCEDURES

2.1 ACTIVATION AND NOTIFICATION

All BC Teams will be notified and activated following a disaster that interrupts normal business operations.

Some situations may require additional assessment to determine the need to activate business continuity plans. In such cases, the BCT may be put on alert. In an alert situation, all BCT members will be notified of the situation, begin preparations for possible activation of the *department/business unit's* Business Continuity Plan, and wait for further information.

For obvious emergencies that interrupt power and/or communications or are otherwise likely to interrupt normal business operations for an extended period, the BCT Leader will report to his/her usual work location as soon as safely possible following the event.

In the event that the usual work location is unusable or inaccessible, the *(Corporate Business Continuity Manager or other designated position)* or his or her designee or alternate will contact all *department/business unit's* BCT Leaders to advise them of the current status and actions to be taken, such as *report to the alternate company location or contracted alternate work area facility*, or wait for further instructions.

For non-obvious emergencies, the *(Corporate Business Continuity Manager or other designated position)* or his or her designee or alternate will assign available staff to notify all *department/business unit* BCT Leaders by telephone or other available means of where and when to report.

(Name of Dept. or Business Unit) Business Continuity Plan File Path (C:\Administrator\ MyDocuments\.......)

Date of Last Revision: 0-00-00

Basic Plan: Page 8 of 22

Company Name   Department/Business Unit Name
Logo   Sample Business Continuity Plan

For either obvious or non-obvious events, the *department/ business unit* BCT Leader or his or her designee will contact all *department/business units'* BCT Team members to advise them:

→ That the Business Continuity Plan has been activated

→ Where and when to report

The *department/business unit* maintains an up-to-date roster of all *business unit/department* employees and their home phone numbers, cell phone numbers, work and personal e-mail addresses, and other contact information such as PDA and pager numbers to assist in the notification process. The *department/business unit* Manager will review and update the list not less than quarterly and as any changes in contact information and/or staffing occur. A copy of the current list is Attachment H to this plan.

While not intended as a method of activating business continuity teams, another source of emergency information is *XYZ*'s designated toll-free emergency phone lines where employees can call to hear emergency information following a major emergency or disaster. A recorded message will provide current, accurate information and also include a time to call the line again for updated information. The numbers are:

→ Primary emergency number for employees: *(area code/ number)*

→ Backup emergency number for employees: *(area code/ number)*

All employees are provided with a laminated card containing these numbers.

Include information and procedures for any other emergency contact systems used by the organization or the business unit/ department such as a calling tree or an electronic notification system.

2.2   SITUATION ASSESSMENT

The BCT Leader will assess the impacts of the event on the *department/business unit*'s most time-critical business functions. Based on the situation and, if applicable, the time in the business cycle, specific restoration strategies will be implemented. As requested, the BCT Leader will provide the Corporate Business Continuity Team with damage/status information. As requested, the BCT Leader will continue to provide situation updates to the Corporate Business Continuity Team.

2.3   BCT INITIAL BRIEFING

Upon arrival at the usual work location or alternate work area location, *department/business unit* BCT Leaders will advise the Corporate Business Continuity Team *(liaison)* of their arrival. Each BCT Leader should immediately begin a log of actions taken; this log will be maintained during the course of the disaster.

A representative of the Corporate BCT will review with *department/business unit* BCT Leaders the status of facilities, utilities, computer systems, communications systems, and operations. To the maximum extent possible, the anticipated duration of any utility outages, computer systems downtime, or other disruptions will also be reported. Any available information

Company Name Logo	Department/Business Unit Name Sample Business Continuity Plan

---

on restoration alternatives and strategies will also be presented to the BCT Leaders.

Each *department/business unit*'s BCT Leader will assess the impact of the disruption(s) on business activities, focusing initially on preestablished time-critical business functions. Short- and long-term impacts of the disruption to operations will be determined and assessments will be reported at an initial briefing with a representative of the Corporate BCT. Based on the existing situation, the *department/business unit* BCT will develop a plan of immediate actions to begin restoring time-critical functions within designated time frames.

2.4 CONTINUITY PRIORITIES

Recovery time objectives (RTOs) have been designated for all business functions based on completion of *XYZ Corporation*'s most recent Business Impact Analysis (BIA). As identified by the BIA, this *department/business unit*'s most time-critical business functions are:

Priority Continuity Order	Time-Critical Business Function	Recovery Time Objective
1		
2		
3		
4		
5		
6		

(Name of Dept. or Business Unit) Business Continuity Plan File Path (C:\Administrator\ MyDocuments\.......)

Date of Last Revision: 0-00-00

Basic Plan: Page 11 of 22

Company Name   Department/Business Unit Name
Logo   Sample Business Continuity Plan

7		
8		
9		
10		
11		

Maximum allowable downtime for some of the listed functions is determined in part by the business cycle requirements as noted below.

(1) End of each business day

(2) End of each business day

(3) Quarterly reports to regulators due within 5 days of quarter end

(4) No downtime in September

(5) Must be completed by 1st Thursday of month

2.5 RESTORATION TIME FRAMES

In *XYZ's* Business Continuity Plan, the most time-critical business functions are assigned a recovery time objective of 72 hours or less. The *department/business unit's* BCT will initiate restoration activities in accordance with the Business Continuity Plan, focusing initially on the most time-critical functions.

2.6 CONTINUITY STRATEGIES AND PROCEDURES

It must be recognized that a significant disruption to normal business activities will require extraordinary measures to en-

Company Name	Department/Business Unit Name
Logo	Sample Business Continuity Plan

sure that predesignated time-critical business functions are continued or restored at a minimal acceptable level. This may necessitate temporary suspension of nonessential functions, relocation of designated personnel to *another company location or a contracted alternate work area*, and/or establishing shift schedules for performing the time-critical business functions.

Strategies to be employed will be based upon the status of utilities, network systems, communications, facilities, and all external supply chain links as well as the anticipated duration of any outages. The preferred strategy would be to restore essential business functions at the normal work location, provided that restoration can be accomplished safely within the designated restoration time frames.

Other strategies may need to be implemented when the time required to regain access and complete restoration of the normal work location will exceed designated restoration time frames, or if extensive recovery activities are required.

This Business Continuity Plan is in coordination with the company's Disaster Recovery Plan, which details restoration strategies for essential support systems such as voice and data communications, network servers, and applications, and for retrieval of off-site electronic records.

2.6.1   Relocation

Relocation is the primary strategy to be employed when the *(office, distribution center, warehouse)* location is rendered unusable or inaccessible and cannot be restored within the target restoration time frames.

(Name of Dept. or Business Unit) Business Continuity Plan File Path (C:\Administrator\ MyDocuments\.......)

Date of Last Revision: 0-00-00

Basic Plan: Page 13 of 22

Company Name   Department/Business Unit Name
Logo   Sample Business Continuity Plan

When a disaster declaration—a formal announcement by preauthorized personnel that a disaster or severe outage is predicted or has occurred—is made, employees designated to continue the most time-critical business functions will be relocated to the contracted alternate work area site. In the event a widespread disaster impacts the primary alternate work area site as well as the usual work location, operations will be relocated to the second alternate work area.

2.6.2 Temporary Suspension

Nonessential business functions may be temporarily suspended if normal work sites are unusable.

2.6.3 Temporary Contracting and Outsourcing

In the event of a long-term disaster-caused disruption to operations or significant damage to facilities, strategies can include temporarily contracting or outsourcing some preidentified time-critical functions. This can include services, processes, warehousing, or distribution. When contracting and outsourcing is identified as a possible strategy, the company's standard procurement process applies and is completed as part of strategy development.

Attachment D contains detailed strategies and procedures for continuing each of the *department/business unit*'s identified time-critical business functions.

(Name of Dept. or Business Unit) Business Continuity Plan File Path (C:\Administrator\ MyDocuments\.......)

Date of Last Revision: 0-00-00

Basic Plan: Page 14 of 22

Company Name
Logo

Department/Business Unit Name
Sample Business Continuity Plan

2.7 SITUATION TRACKING

The *department/business unit* BCT Leader will track the progress of the *department/business unit's* continuation or restoration of its time-critical business functions and will report current status information in writing to the *(Corporate liaison)* on a schedule determined by the Corporate Business Continuity Team. A Business Continuity Status Report Form is included in Attachment F.

2.8 EMPLOYEE INFORMATION

In the event of a potential or actual disaster event, information will be disseminated to all department employees by the Business Continuity Team Leader.

A complete, current contact list for all *department/business unit* employees will be maintained in this plan as Attachment H. The list will be reviewed and revised not less than quarterly and more often as required by any changes in personnel.

2.9 LONG-TERM RECOVERY

A major disaster may cause damages to facilities requiring major repair or reconstruction lasting months or possibly even years. The Corporate Business Continuity Team will coordinate the long-term recovery effort to restore operations and services to pre-disaster levels and to adapt services to changed conditions brought about by the disaster with *department/business unit* Business Continuity Team Leaders.

(Name of Dept. or Business Unit) Business Continuity Plan File Path (C:\Administrator\ MyDocuments\.......)

Date of Last Revision: 0-00-00

Basic Plan: Page 15 of 22

Company Name   Department/Business Unit Name

Logo   Sample Business Continuity Plan

2.10 TRACKING CONTINUITY COSTS

For insurance purposes, it is essential to keep detailed records of damages and expenditures. Each *department/business unit* BCT will implement procedures for tracking the number of disaster-related hours worked and any other related costs and expenditures.

The *department/business unit's* BCT Leader must ensure that all insurance-required expense records are fully and accurately maintained. These records will be provided to the *(Corporate BCT liaison)* as requested. A sample Business Continuity Expense Tracking Form is included in this plan as Attachment I.

2.11 DEPARTMENT CONTINUITY STRATEGIES

2.11.1 Asset Protection

Describe actions that will be taken to protect assets in your department such as preassigning employees to remove and/or secure identified assets such as petty cash, check stock, confidential records, and inventory in the event that the work location must be evacuated. (Include a caveat that these actions are to be taken only if doing so in no way endangers the safety of employees.)

2.11.2 Vital Records Protection & Reconstruction

Identify the vital records needed to perform time-critical business functions, including alternate sources for such records. Develop and implement procedures for secur-

---

(Name of Dept. or Business Unit) Business Continuity Plan File Path (C:\Administrator\ MyDocuments\.......)

Date of Last Revision: 0-00-00

Basic Plan: Page 16 of 22

ing, off-site storage, retrieval and reconstruction of vital records—electronic and non-electronic, as necessary.

2.11.3 Essential Systems and Applications

The following systems and applications are required to continue or restore *department/business unit's* identified critical functions. The recovery time objective (RTO) listed for each is based on the IT Department's Disaster Recovery Plan.

System/Application	RTO	System/Application	RTO

2.11.4 Resource Needs

Individual alternate work area site workstations are equipped with a standard PC, basic telephone, a shared printer, and basic office supplies. Unless required due to confidentiality requirements, all copy machines and facsimile machines will be shared.

In addition to the standard equipment, the *department/business unit* will require special equipment, nonstandard hardware or printers, forms, manuals, directories, and phones listed in Attachment J.

(Name of Dept. or Business Unit) Business Continuity Plan File Path (C:\Administrator\ MyDocuments\.......)

Date of Last Revision: 0-00-00

Basic Plan: Page 17 of 22

Company Name	Department/Business Unit Name
Logo	Sample Business Continuity Plan

(As applicable) The department has gathered and stored off-site at (location) certain essential forms, manuals, procedures, directories, resource lists, etc., required by the department's time-critical functions. Attachment J includes an inventory list of the contents. Contents are inventoried and updated following every test, exercise, and actual disaster but not less than annually or as needed, and the inventory list is updated accordingly.

A list of all *critical suppliers, outsourcing companies, shippers, vendors, contractors, and other business partners* necessary to fulfill the identified time-critical functions, and where applicable alternates for each with complete contact information, is provided in Attachment K. This list includes company names, contact names, and all available contact information. The *department/business unit* BCT Leader is responsible for ensuring that the list is reviewed and updated not less than quarterly.

2.11.5 Staffing and Scheduling

The minimum acceptable level of staffing needed to perform time-critical business functions has been identified and is found in Attachment A. Staffing includes one primary and two backup persons for each continuity assignment.

In addition, all BCT members will assist and back up one another as required to continue or restore the identified critical functions.

In the event of an extended BC time frame, the *department/business unit* BC Leader will identify and assign

(Name of Dept. or Business Unit) Business Continuity Plan File Path (C:\Administrator\ MyDocuments\.......)

Date of Last Revision: 0-00-00

Basic Plan: Page 18 of 22

Company Name
Logo

Department/Business Unit Name
Sample Business Continuity Plan

---

staff and designate shift work schedules if necessary and feasible. All scheduling will take into account the current point in related business cycles.

2.11.6 Notification and Recall

The *department/business unit's* Team Leader will notify all *department/business unit* BC Team members in the event of a disaster. Information provided will be a brief description of the type of disaster; its impact on facilities, services, and operations; when and where Team members are to report; current contact information for the *department/business unit* Business Continuity Leader; and other pertinent information. If Team members are not to immediately report to the alternate work area, an estimated time for an updated status will be provided.

When Team members report to the alternate work area, they should be prepared to present picture identification *(insert necessary instructions for entry into alternate work locations)*. Entry into the work area is not permitted without valid picture identification.

2.11.7 Business Continuity Procedures

Attachment D contains detailed specific procedures for each employee who has a business continuity assignment. In addition, an action checklist for each assignment is included in Attachment L.

(Name of Dept. or Business Unit) Business Continuity Plan File Path (C:\Administrator\ MyDocuments\.......)

Date of Last Revision: 0-00-00

Basic Plan: Page 19 of 22

Company Name	Department/Business Unit Name
Logo	Sample Business Continuity Plan

2.12 DEACTIVATION

The *department/business unit*'s Business Continuity Team will continue operations at the usual workplace *or (alternate company location or the contracted alternate work area location)* until a decision to deactivate the Business Continuity Plan is made by the Corporate Business Continuity Team. *Department/business unit* BCT Leaders will be notified of the decision and date(s) of deactivation and specific deactivation instructions.

Deactivation procedures for all departments will be scheduled and coordinated by the Corporate Business Continuity Team. The detailed business continuity procedures for each time-critical function include the deactivation process.

Immediately following deactivation of Business Continuity Plans, each Business Continuity Team Leader will conduct a full debrief with all team members to capture the lessons learned and submit a written report to the *Corporate Business Continuity Team or Corporate Business Continuity Manager*. A full debrief with all *department/business unit* Business Continuity Team Leaders will be conducted by the Corporate Business Continuity Team. The purpose of the debriefing process is to identify areas for improvement to ensure that necessary corrective actions are taken.

2.13 TRAINING AND TESTING

To provide training to all Business Continuity Team members, the *department/business unit*'s BCP will be tested twice annually: one tabletop exercise and one scheduled alternate work area test. The tabletop exercise will be conducted by the *department/business unit* BC Leader; the alternate work area test

---

(Name of Dept. or Business Unit) Business Continuity Plan File Path (C:\Administrator\ MyDocuments\.......)

Date of Last Revision: 0-00-00

Basic Plan: Page 20 of 22

will be coordinated by *(Corporate Business Continuity Manager or owner of Corporate BCP)*. Business Continuity Plans will be revised and updated as necessary based on lessons learned during each test and exercise.

Each *department/business unit* Manager will review plan basics with all employees at least annually and document the review in writing to the *(Corporate Business Continuity Manager or owner of Corporate BCP)*.

2.14 PLAN REVIEW AND REVISION

At the direction of the Department Manager, the *department/ business unit's* BC Leader will be responsible for the maintenance and update of this plan. The plan will be reviewed and updated not less than annually and by not later than *(date)* of each year. In addition, interim review and revisions will be completed when needed as a result of changes that may impact continuity procedures such as department/business unit processes, staffing, location, and suppliers. The date of the most recent revision will be printed in the bottom right-hand corner of each page of the document.

To assist with the annual review and update, a planning session for all *department/business unit* BCT Leaders will be conducted by the *(Corporate Business Continuity Manager or owner of Corporate BCP)*.

Additional revisions will be made as required by changes in the department necessitating revisions in the basic plan or any of its attachments. A copy of all plan updates will be sent to the *(Corporate Business Continuity Manager or owner of Corporate BCP)* via e-mail. An audit record of all plan revisions and updates will be maintained on the Plan Review and Revisions form found at the front of this plan, and all existing copies of the plan (hard copies and electronic files) will be updated.

To ensure that all holders of the plan receive all updates and revisions, each hard copy of the *department/business unit's* Business Continuity Plan will be numbered. The plan distribution record found at the front of this plan will be maintained to accurately identify those who hold copies of the plan.

In addition to the copies maintained at the department level, hard and soft copies will be maintained by the *(Corporate Business Continuity Manager or owner of the Corporate BCP)*, and a hard copy will be maintained at *(alternate company location, contracted alternate work area site, or other off-site location)*.

(Name of Dept. or Business Unit) Business Continuity Plan File Path (C:\Administrator\ MyDocuments\.......)   Date of Last Revision: 0-00-00

Basic Plan: Page 22 of 22

Glossary

activation Putting into motion all or a portion of a business continuity plan and its teams and procedures in response to a disaster.

assumptions Basic understandings about potential disaster situations upon which a business continuity plan and/or disaster recovery plan is based.

brand A name, symbol, or logo that represents a company, product, or service and makes the company, product, or service recognizable to customers and the public.

business continuity A proactive approach to ensure continuity or rapid restoration of delivery of the organization's service or product following a disaster. The ability of an organization to provide service and support for its customers and to maintain its viability before, during, and after a disaster. Also referred to as *business restoration, business recovery,* or *business resumption.*

business continuity center (BCC) A facility or portion of a facility designed to serve as an operational center for a business continuity team to centralize and manage the business continuity process. A BCC can be located on or off the organization's premises.

business continuity management (BCM) An ongoing enterprise-wide holistic management process that identifies risks and potential impacts that threaten an organization and its operations. Also provides a framework for building resilience and the capability for an effective response that safeguards the interests of the organization and its key stakeholders, reputation, brand, and value.

business continuity planning A process to develop, implement, and maintain strategies and procedures to ensure that key operations and essential business functions can continue or quickly be restored in the event of a disaster, state of emergency, or significant threat to the organization and its operations.

business continuity planning lifecycle A process of continuity planning that includes the development, maintenance, and testing of business continuity plans to ensure a continually maintained and enhanced business continuity program. Specific ongoing lifecycle steps include hazard assessment and mitigation, business impact analysis, development of business continuity strategies, development of business continuity plans and procedures, training, testing and exercising of developed plans, as well as ongoing efforts to maintain and improve the program.

business continuity program (BCP) A comprehensive, proactive, ongoing set of activities with the specific goal of developing and maintaining the capability of a company or other organization to respond to a serious emergency or disaster event that interrupts or threatens to interrupt normal business operations.

business impact analysis (BIA) A methodology and process used to identify the effects a disaster may have on a business and to identify, quantify, and prioritize time-critical business functions throughout the organization. The BIA identifies maximum allowable downtime, sequence of restoration and staffing requirements, support systems, special equipment, and other resources required by each critical business function, as well as the interdependencies among internal business units and dependencies outside the organization. BIA results are used as a guide in developing business continuity strategies and plans.

checklist A list of specific step-by-step actions taken by a member of the business continuity team or other related team in response to a particular disaster event or significant interruption of operations.

Continuity of Operations (COOP) plan The term used by government agencies to fulfill the requirement that all agencies have in place a viable COOP capability that ensures the performance of their essential functions during any emergency or situation that may disrupt normal operations. The counterpart in the private sector is a *business continuity plan*.

coordination A planned approach to working together and sharing critical resources. The extent to which organizations attempt to ensure that their activities take into account those of other organizations. Organizations' deliberate degree of adjustment to one another.

crate and ship A contractual arrangement with an equipment vendor or supplier to ship replacement equipment within a specified time period following notification in order to facilitate a strategy for making critical equipment available following a disaster.

crisis An event that threatens life, property, or business operations beyond acceptable losses if not controlled. A turning point for better or worse, a crucial time, a decisive moment.

critical function A business activity that is essential to avoid significantly jeopardizing the organization's ability to operate at an acceptable level. Any task or operation the loss or unavailability of which would have a catastrophic impact on the successful conduct of business. Also referred to as a *vital business function* or *time-critical business function*.

customer An individual, company, or organization that purchases or otherwise receives a service or product from another individual, company, or organization.

damage assessment The process of assessing damage following a disaster to determine what equipment, records, facilities, infrastructure, and inventory can be salvaged or restored and what must be replaced. A damage assessment can also provide an initial estimate of the length of time required to restore operations.

disaster A destructive or disruptive event, usually sudden or unexpected, beyond the response capabilities of the organizations where it has occurred. Typically brings great damage, loss, or destruction. For businesses, any event—large or small—that causes a cessation of vital business functions; an event requiring immediate action to ensure continuation or resumption of operations. Also referred to as a *disaster event* or *event*. Note: Based on its impact on operations, an event that may be only a nuisance for one company could be a disaster for another. See also **event**.

disaster recovery The restoration of an organization's technology to provide the IT, telecommunications, and related technology needed to support business continuity objectives.

distributor An entity that sells a product or variety of products to customers. A company or individual who buys products, warehouses them, and resells and ships them to retailers or directly to end users.

downstream That part of the supply chain between producers of products or services and their end customers. Downstream links include distributors, wholesalers, and retailers.

emergency An urgent situation, a condition of disaster, or a condition of extreme peril to the safety of persons and property. Emergencies can be large or small.

emergency response team (ERT) Teams of designated employees organized, trained, and equipped to respond to emergencies occurring at the organization's facilities by providing assistance to employees and visitors and, as required, directing building evacuation.

enterprise resource planning (ERP) An integrated information system, evolved from Manufacturing Resource Planning (MRP) II, that serves all departments within an enterprise to coordinate manufacturing processes to enterprise-wide back-end processes. ERP software is a multi-module application software that integrates activities across departments and can include product planning, parts purchasing, inventory control, distribution, and order tracking; it may also include application modules for finance, accounting, and human resources functions.

event An occurrence, often happening suddenly, that may cause damage to facilities or infrastructure, disruption of operations, or even loss of human life. Results are often a serious disruption of the functioning of an organization and possible material, economic, or environmental losses. See also **disaster**.

exercise An activity designed to promote business continuity preparedness. A process to evaluate business continuity and related operations plans, procedures, or facilities. Training for personnel assigned to business continuity and other disaster-related duties. Used as a means to test business continuity strategies, plans, and procedures. Three basic exercise categories are tabletop, simulation, and live.

Federal Emergency Management Agency (FEMA) U.S. government agency, formerly independent, that became part of the Department of Homeland Security in March 2003. Tasked with responding to, planning for, recovering from, and mitigating against disasters and for supporting disaster preparedness, response, and recovery efforts at the state and local government level. The beginnings of FEMA can be traced to the Congressional Act of 1803.

hazard Any source of damage or element of risk. A situation or condition with potential for loss or harm. Any event that will deny an organization the use of its normal work area or the connectivity or access to that area. Three basic types of hazards are natural, technological, and human-caused.

hazard assessment Identification of the most probable threats and the analysis of the related impacts of the identified threats. The evaluation of existing physical and environmental security and controls in combination with assessing existing capability to manage the potential threats to the organization. See also **risk analysis**.

hazardous material (hazmat incident) Any uncontrolled release of a material capable of posing a risk to health and safety and property. The hazardous material may be stationary or in transit. (1) Stationary: Areas at risk include facilities that produce, process, or store hazardous material as well as all sites that treat, store, and dispose of hazardous material. (2) In transit: Any spill during transport of material by land, waterways, or air that is potentially a risk to health and safety.

homeland security A concerted national effort to prevent terrorist attacks within the United States, reduce the nation's vulnerability to terrorism, and minimize the damage and recover from attacks that do occur. A federal government agency, the Department of Homeland Security (DHS), is charged with carrying out the homeland security goals and has primary responsibility for ensuring that emergency response professionals are prepared for any situation. DHS also provides a coordinated, comprehensive federal response to any large-scale crisis or disaster. Includes the *Federal Emergency Management Agency (FEMA)*.

hot site A remote, redundant (backup) computer operations location equipped with compatible hardware and the infrastructure needed to support operations. A fully operational data processing facility configured to an organization's specifications, usually available beginning within a few hours of a disaster. Some have adjacent furnished office space and support facilities. A company may establish its own hot site at another company location, or a hot site may be contracted with a vendor; a reciprocal agreement with another company is yet another alternative. Also referred to as *backup site, recovery site, recovery center,* or *alternate processing site*.

Incident Command System (ICS) A management system for responding to and controlling an emergency or disaster caused by natural, technological, or human-caused events. The system was developed by public safety agencies and is now the nationally used standardized on-scene emergency management concept. ICS includes five parts: command/direction, operations, planning, logistics, and finance.

information technology (IT) Resources and systems used to collect and organize data and information used to conduct business. The business unit or department responsible for managing computer systems and related technology.

infrastructure A general term used to describe all systems for storing, treating, and distributing fuel, communications, water, wastewater, and electricity. By some definitions may include roadways, bridges, etc. Also referred to as *lifelines*.

intermodal shipping Transporting shipments using more than one method of transportation. For example, a shipment may be carried in shipping containers on a tractor trailer, transferred to rail flat cars for transit to a ship or barge, then to a truck for final delivery.

inventory Raw materials, components, or parts stored for use in the production process or finished goods or finished products stored before being shipped to a customer or to a distributor.

ISO (International Organization for Standardization) A global network of national standards institutes of approximately 160 countries coordinated by a Central Secretariat in Geneva, Switzerland. ISO provides standards and guidelines for quality in the manufacturing and service industries and is the world's largest developer and publisher of quality management system standards, technical specifications, technical reports, handbooks, and web-based documents on quality management. Note: Because the acronyms for "International Organization for Standardization" would be different in different languages (IOS in English, OIN in French for *Organisation internationale de normalisation*), the group's founders gave it a short, all-purpose name ISO, derived from the Greek *isos*, meaning "equal."

just-in-time (JIT) A methodology that creates the movement of material into a specific location at a specified time, usually just before the material is needed in a manufacturing process. An inventory management philosophy aimed at improving responsiveness, reducing costs, and reducing waste and excess inventory by delivering products, components, or materials just when they are needed.

logistics (1) *Supply chain*: All elements of the supply chain coordinated to plan, implement, and control the upstream and downstream flow (purchasing, production, distribution) of goods, services, and information beginning with the point of origin and ending with the point of final consumption with a goal of meeting customer requirements. (2) *Business continuity*: Derived from the Incident Command System (ICS), a branch of the emergency response or business continuity team that is activated following a disaster declaration, typically staffed by representatives of departments associated with supply acquisition and material transportation. Responsible for ensuring the most effective acquisition and mobilization of supplies and materials necessary to support business continuity strategies. May also be responsible for transporting and supporting staff with business continuity responsibilities.

Manufacturing Resource Planning (MRP II) A computer-based management tool that expands on MRP I to include other functions throughout the company such as marketing and finance.

Material Requirements Planning (MRP I) A computer-based management tool that provides a manufacturer with a means of determining what products to produce and in what quantities, based on the response to what the manufacturer sells to its customers.

metrics In a business context, any type of measurement used to gauge a quantifiable component of an organization's performance. For example, a company's return on investment (ROI) is a metric used to quantify profit.

mitigation Pre-event planning and actions that aim to eliminate or lessen the effects of potential disasters. Actions taken well in advance of a destructive or disruptive event to reduce, avoid, or protect against its impacts. Must be an ongoing process to manage changes.

outsourcing Strategic use of resources outside the organization to carry out functions previously performed by internal staff and resources. The contracting out of major functions to specialized providers that may be more efficient or cost-effective.

pandemic A disease affecting a whole population or a number of countries. A global epidemic. An outbreak of an infectious disease that affects people or animals over an extensive geographical area.

Pareto Principle Named after Italian economist Vilfredo Pareto, a principle that specifies an unequal relationship between inputs and outputs. The principle states that, for many phenomena, 20 percent of invested input is responsible for 80 percent of the results obtained; 80 percent of consequences are the result of 20 percent of the causes. Also referred to as the *Pareto rule* or *80-20 Rule*.

partnership A tailored business relationship based on mutual trust, openness, shared risk, and shared rewards that yields a competitive advantage, resulting in business performance greater for both or all parties than would be achieved by the individual entities.

pick and pack Part of the supply chain management process used in the distribution of goods. The process may be manual or computerized. (1) *Pick*: Small or large quantities of merchandise are picked from a warehouse to fulfill customer orders for specific destinations. (2) *Pack*: Picked merchandise is packaged for shipment to specific locations with an invoice enclosed and a shipping label affixed.

prodrome An event showing that a disaster could result under slightly different circumstances. A warning sign. Derived from the Greek for "running before."

public information officer (PIO) An individual responsible for all media contact on behalf of the organization and to whom all media requests for information are referred. The PIO's duties can include preparing press releases, conducting media briefings, and arranging for press conferences.

reciprocal agreement A formal agreement made by two or more companies or organizations to share or use each other's resources following a disaster.

recovery Short- and long-term activities to return operations to normal. Recovery requires well-developed strategies to enable timely and orderly continuation or restoration of operations. See **business continuity**.

recovery point objective (RPO) The point in time to which systems and data must be recovered and restored after an outage (e.g., the end of the previous day's processing) in order to resume processing. RPOs are often used as the basis for the development of backup strategies and as a determinant of the amount of data that must be recreated after the systems or functions have been recovered.

recovery time objective (RTO) The period of time within which systems, applications, or functions must be recovered after an outage (e.g., thirty minutes or less, twenty-four hours or less, seventy-two hours or less). RTOs are often used as the basis for the development of business continuity and disaster recovery strategies. Also referred to as *maximum allowable downtime* or *maximum allowable outage*.

redundant/redundancy The provision of more than one means or resource for performing a function. From a business continuity and/or disaster recovery perspective, redundancy refers to the duplication of critical equipment or systems—such as telecommunications, information systems, manufacturing equipment, skills, resources, suppliers, or facilities—to help ensure that the organization can continue or quickly resume operations when a disaster occurs.

resilience The capacity of a system or organization to absorb disruption and still preserve its basic structure and function. The ability of individuals, organizations, or other entities to anticipate and respond proactively to disruption, adversity, or significant change.

resilient Able to recover rapidly from adversity.

response Immediate actions taken during or immediately following a destructive or disruptive event to reduce impacts or to stop its effects.

restoration The activities needed to restore a facility or processing capability to its normal condition. Restoration involves the steps necessary to plan, organize, and continue these activities.

reverse logistics A supply chain process to handle the return of orders and packaging. Handling product returns back through the supply chain. The process of moving goods from their final destination for the purpose of capturing value or for proper disposal. Processing returns for any reason such as damage, excessive inventory, seasonal inventory, recalls, or salvage.

risk analysis Identification of the most probable threats and the analysis of the related vulnerabilities of the organization to these threats. Evaluation of existing physical and environmental security and controls, and assessing their adequacy relative to the potential threats to the organization. Also referred to as *risk assessment, impact assessment, corporate loss analysis, risk identification,* and *exposure assessment.*

risk management A process to help organizations understand, evaluate, and take action on all their risks in order to increase the probability of success and reduce the likelihood of failure or an unacceptable level of loss. A process to identify and control all risks to help ensure that the organization will continue to fulfill its mission.

Sarbanes-Oxley Act (SOX) A U.S. law passed in 2002 establishing a broad range of standards for public companies, their boards, and accounting firms. It was designed to increase corporate accountability through specific reporting requirements that companies and their executive boards must follow. The law, which is overseen by the Securities and Exchange Commission (SEC), requires infrastructure to preserve and protect information, records, and data.

scenario A brief narrative describing a hypothetical situation and conditions and the likely future when a destructive or disruptive event occurs. Beginning with a believable event, a scenario identifies the managerial setting and physical conditions and describes the impacts. Essential for preparedness planning, scenarios are also used as a basis for continuity exercises.

service level agreement (SLA) A legally binding contract or formal agreement between a supplier and a customer that details the nature, quality, and scope of the service or product to be provided. An agreement between a customer and the provider of a service or product that covers detailed specifications for the level and quality of service or product to be delivered.

stakeholder An individual, organization, or specific interest group that believes he/she or it will be impacted by the actions or inaction of another individual, organization, or specific interest group organization.

strategic planning A process that assesses the probable divergent scenarios and addresses what policies the organization should adopt to mitigate adverse impacts, prepare for the scenarios in the short term, respond, take advantage of opportunities each scenario may present, restore functions when impacts occur, and recover or change over a long time frame after a scenario occurs.

strategy An approach and course of action developed by an organization to ensure its recovery and continuity in the face of a disaster or other major operational interruption. Business continuity and/or disaster recovery plans and methodologies are determined by and support the organization's strategy.

supplier risk analysis A hazard assessment or risk analysis of an organization's suppliers, vendors, outsourcing companies, or contractors to identify and understand their risks and vulnerabilities and related ability to continue to deliver their product or service on time at an acceptable level of quality when disaster strikes.

supply chain A network of organizations that brings products or services to market through the exchange of resources including materials and information. The management of a network of interconnected businesses and processes involved in the ultimate delivery of products and services required by end customers. Spans and includes all activities and relationships—upstream and downstream—relating to the acquisition, movement, and storage of goods and services from the point of origin to the final delivery location. A supply chain consists of a company or organization and its suppliers, distributors, outsourcing companies, and customers. Also referred to as *value chain*.

supply chain management (SCM) Management of the processes that get the right things to the right places at the right time, typically with a goal of making a profit. Actionable strategies to optimize supply chain operations. Integration, coordination, and management of a network of interconnected companies and business processes from end user through original suppliers that provides products, services, and information that add value for customers.

tabletop exercise An exercise where participants walk through a response to a disaster situation, typically using only the plan document. This type of exercise provides a nonstressful way to train people and test plan documents while providing a team-building opportunity for business continuity team members. Also referred to as a *walkthrough exercise* or *desktop exercise*.

terrorism Systematic use of terror or unpredictable violence against governments, populations, or individuals, usually to attain a political objective.

threat Anything that can have a direct or indirect harmful effect on an organization or its operations.

uninterruptible power supply (UPS) An alternate short-term power supply, usually battery powered, to maintain power in the event of an electrical power outage. Typically, a UPS keeps computers or other equipment operating for several minutes after a power outage, enabling a graceful shutdown. Some UPS units include software that automates backup and shutdown procedures in the event of a power loss.

upstream That part of a supply chain between the producers of a service or product(s) and their suppliers of raw materials, parts, components, processes, or services that are used in manufacturing or creating their product(s).

value stream Activities within a supply chain that add value, especially in the estimation of the customer.

vital records Documents or records, paper or electronic, which—for legal, regulatory, or operational reasons—cannot be lost or damaged without impairing the organization's ability to successfully conduct business.

work-around procedures Interim manual procedures that may be used by a business unit to enable it to continue to perform its critical business functions during temporary unavailability of specific computer applications, computerized systems, electronic or hard copy data, or voice or data communication.

worst-case scenario The maximum intensity of a specific hazard, coupled with the maximum estimated impact on operations. For most hazards, the highest impact will be associated with a disaster that is less likely to occur.

Index